A Biblical Response to Environmental Issues
Calvin B. DeWitt

EARTH-WISE

P9-DFM-088

CRC Publications
Grand Rapids, Michigan

Earth-Wise
A Biblical Response to Environmental Issues
Copyright © 1994 by CRC Publications, 2850 Kalamazoo SE, Grand Rapids, Michigan 49560.

Library of Congress Cataloging-in-Publication Data
DeWitt, Calvin B.
    Earth wise: a biblical response to environmental issues / Calvin B. DeWitt.
        p. cm. — (Issues in Christian living)
    Includes bibliographical references.
    ISBN 1-56212-057-3 (TBA)
    1. Nature—Biblical teaching. 2. Human ecology—Biblical teaching. 3. Stewardship, Christian. I. Title. II. Series.
BS660.D48   1993
261.8'362—dc20
                                   94-6513
                                     CIP

10 9 8 7 6 5 4 3 2

CONTENTS

PREFACE

Environmental issues are much in the news. We hear of air and water pollution, of global warming, and of the threatened extinction of numerous species of animal and vegetable life. These are alarming matters.

How do we react? Some of us join crusades to save the snail darter or the rain forests. Others angrily protest such crusades as threats to our livelihoods. Most remain uninvolved, trusting that somehow the scientists and governments will solve these problems for us. But what should the Christian stance be? That's the question this book tries to answer.

The author of *Earth-Wise,* Calvin B. DeWitt, is a lifelong environmentalist; professor of Environmental Studies at the University of Wisconsin-Madison; director of the Au Sable Institute of Environmental Studies located in Mancelona, Michigan; and participant in several Christian studies on this matter. In this book DeWitt presents a careful, balanced summary of the main environmental issues that face us today. He does this in the consistent awareness that we are talking about God's creation—not just our human habitat. Accordingly, we should not panic at threats to the environment since its final maintenance and care rests in God's divine hands.

As stewards of creation, however, we are responsible to God to think about what consequences our actions have for the environment. We are charged by God to keep and care for creation. As faithful stewards, we must raise awareness of environmental issues in our churches and communities and reflect that awareness in our own patterns of daily living.

We offer this book for your reading, reflection, and possible discussion, trusting that it will aid in some small way to make us all better environmental stewards, people who lovingly and joyfully care for God's good creation.

Harvey A. Smit
Editor in chief
Education Department

INTRODUCTION

I have been in love with the Creator since my childhood and have been inspired and awed by God's creation for over fifty years. I gained an early appreciation for God's creatures from caring for and keeping the animals in the backyard zoo of my childhood and youth.

I am now a teacher. I have taught thousands of college and university students (and nearly every other person I've ever met), helping them to develop a profound sense of awe and wonder for God's world. Like the great Teacher—my model—I too like to teach on field trips! And, I am also a continuous student, learning from the "university of creation" and from God's holy Word.

One Sunday evening when I was in my teens, I overheard my uncle ask my dad a question about me: "Shouldn't you help Cal do something more important than this—something that will help him get a job?" My dad guided him down the basement stairs to see my birds and fish while my mom and aunt prepared after-church coffee and goodies. Then my dad responded to my uncle's question, softly replying that he thought I was doing just fine. You see, my dad had told me earlier to keep doing what I loved to do; that would mean I would do it very well, and doing it very well meant that eventually someone would even pay me for it. In this—his rendition of Matthew 6:33—he was ever so right! I now get paid for what I love to do. My profession is caring for God's creation and helping others to do so too.

Early on, some of the people I talked to about my work saw it as leading nowhere. Later, as I studied at Calvin College and the University of

Michigan, many people viewed my work with curiosity. Then, much later—during the early 1970s—most people saw my work as being vitally important. As my work developed, it was labeled radical (because it suggested we might have to change the way we lived). But, as environmental fervor grew across the land, people began to see this very same work as too conservative (because I failed to take a stand, among other things, on the ecological unsoundness of pink toilet paper). In the late 1980s that same work was again seen as curious but largely irrelevant. And today? Well, most people think it is important again. What's next? The next stage—I feel it coming—is that what I am doing and saying about the care and keeping of God's creation will again be seen as too radical (for the same reasons as before)!

This book will both lighten the load we carry and give us a great deal of (joyful) redeeming things to do. It will not pile on the guilt. God knows we, and all members of the human race, are guilty—always have been! "For all have sinned and fall short of the glory of God" (Rom. 3:23). But ours is not to grovel in polluted gutters, nor is it to wring our hands over our sins. Instead, our purpose is to go about reclaiming creation for our Lord; for, as Psalm 24:1 tells us, "The earth is the LORD's. . . ." When we work to reclaim God's creation, we do so in joyful gratitude for God's great gift of salvation.

Even now, as we begin by immersing ourselves in understanding creation's degradation, we are uplifted by the certain knowledge of God's rule, of God's loving gift of Jesus—through whom the world was made, by whom the whole world is held together. For Jesus Christ is the one given by God to reconcile all things to himself. We know he is the one we must follow. Jesus never fails. Jesus is our best example of practicing dominion and stewardship.

Come with me now, first into the dark recesses of creation's degradations, soon to surface into the Bible's teachings on the care and keeping of creation, then to ascend into the joyful stewardship of the children of God!

—Calvin B. DeWitt

The earth was given to man, with this condition, that he should occupy himself in its cultivation. . . . The custody of the garden was given in charge to Adam, to show that we possess the things which God has committed to our hands, on the condition that, being content with the frugal and moderate use of them, we should take care of what shall remain. Let him who possesses a field, so partake of its yearly fruits, that he may not suffer the ground to be injured by his negligence, but let him endeavor to hand it down to posterity as he received it, or even better cultivated. Let him so feed on its fruits, that he neither dissipates it by luxury, nor permits it to be marred or ruined by neglect. Moreover, that this economy, and this diligence, with respect to those good things which God has given us to enjoy, may flourish among us; let everyone regard himself as the steward of God in all things which he possesses. Then he will neither conduct himself dissolutely, nor corrupt by abuse those things which God requires to be preserved.

> John Calvin, 1554, *Commentary on Genesis,* from the
> English translation of 1847. As reprinted by Banner
> of Truth Publishers, 1965.

ONE

SEVEN PROVISIONS FOR CREATION[1]

Introduction

I was born and raised in the city of Grand Rapids, Michigan. I have inhabited the great Waubesa Marsh in Wisconsin now for more than twenty years.

It is in many ways easier to learn of the workings of God's creation in this wetland ecosystem, yet the city also provided a wonderful place to learn creation's lessons. There were the torrential rains and gentle drizzles whose drifting wetness I experienced with my brother and sister as we swung on a suspended canvas swing under the roof of our front porch. There was a tornado's immense funnel cloud that once roared menacingly over the roof of Baxter Laundry. There were the nighthawks whose noisy "zzbbrrraaaaaaaaaaaannnggggg!" broke the silence of the summer's night sky as they pulled out from their dramatic plunging dives. There were the bats whose zig-zag flights around the corner streetlight kept our insects in check. And there was Mrs. Lockhart's Dutchman's-pipe, a climbing vine with heart-shaped leaves, on which the pipe vine swallowtail caterpillars ate away with her reluctant approval. These caterpillars eventually became magnificent butterflies that fluttered around the neighborhood or flopped away as they emerged from captivity in my mother's canning jars.

[1] A full treatment of the provisions of the biosphere, in addition to a description of environmental degradations and needed responses, can be found in *Environmental Science: The Way the World Works* by Bernard J. Nebel and Richard T. Wright (Englewood Cliffs, NJ: Prentice-Hall, 1993).

But better still were my bike rides to the dump at the edge of town and into the country where I could find frogs, salamanders, snakes, and turtles. Many of these treasures I brought home to my backyard zoo where I could study them for hours and days on end.

There was no question in my mind about the reason for all this wonderful life. For what I was learning from these beautiful creatures was fully consistent with what I was hearing from sermons in my church and lessons at Baldwin Christian School. All these creatures were God's. They were works of the Master, of the Creator in whom all creatures great and small, his Master-pieces, lived and moved and had their being. They were the ones about whom I sang each Sunday, "Praise God, all creatures here below!"

It was a world that day after day opened new lessons about God's creatures and filled life with reasons for praise. The psalms I sang in church beautifully complemented what I was learning in creation. Remember how Psalm 148 goes, for example? This is the way we used to sing it:

Hallelujah, praise Jehovah,
from the heavens praise his name;
praise Jehovah in the highest,
all his angels, praise proclaim.
All his hosts, together praise him,
sun and moon and stars on high;
praise him, O ye heavens of heavens,
and ye floods above the sky.

And then, in the next verse:

Let them praises give Jehovah,
they were made at his command;
them forever he established,
his decree shall ever stand.
From the earth, O praise Jehovah,
all ye seas, ye monsters all,
fire and hail and snow and vapors,
stormy winds that hear his call.

And with this as the introduction, we then burst forth with everything we had as we sang of trees, frogs, turtles, elephants, Holsteins, Jerseys, birds, kings, and my relatives and neighbors:

All ye fruitful trees and cedars,
all ye hills and mountains high,
creeping things and beasts and cattle,
birds that in the heavens fly,
kings of earth, and all ye people,
princes great, earth's judges all;

praise his name, young men and maidens,
aged men and children small.

Let them praises give Jehovah
for his name alone is high,
and his glory is exalted,
  and his glory is exalted,
    and his glory is exalted,
far above the earth and sky!

Today, when on Sunday evenings our friends and neighbors from around our marsh and from the nearby city of Madison come together, we still sing that very song. And when our singing follows a walk through this wetland, one of my neighbors shouts out, "BIRDS THAT IN THE HEAVENS FLY!"

All creation praises God. Of this I am fully convinced. But beyond that, all creation breaks forth with a marvelous testimony. This testimony leaves everyone without excuse—all who witness creation are confronted with God's everlasting power and the fact that God is God, that God is divine. I remember in my youth savoring the words of Article 2 of the Belgic Confession because it affirmed—in a deep theological way—the worth of my continuous observation of animals and plants in the city, the city dump, and in the country beyond:

Article 2: The Means by Which We Know God

We know him by two means:

First, by the creation, preservation, and government
of the universe,
since that universe is before our eyes
like a beautiful book
  in which all creatures,
  great and small,
  are as letters
  to make us ponder
  the invisible things of God:
    his eternal power
    and his divinity,
    as the apostle Paul says in Romans 1:20.

All these things are enough to convince men
and to leave them without excuse.

Second, he makes himself known to us more openly
by his Holy and divine Word,
as much as we need in this life,
  for his glory
  and for the salvation of his own.

Today as I write this, on Waubesa Marsh, the heavens continue to tell the glory of God, and the creatures continue to pour forth their testimony to God's eternal power and divine majesty.

It is a drizzly day in early spring. The marsh seems expectant, ready to burst forth with all kinds of life. The geese call above, and six sandhill cranes with their clangoring calls announce the arrival and revival of life on the great marsh. All of this brings me to ask: What is it for which creation praises God?

A joyful reading of Psalm 104 will help provide the answer. As we read this psalm, we are assured that God is the great Provider as well as the masterful Creator. God's provisions for life and breath are everywhere evident. And God's provisions are so numerous and so interwoven with each other that we could never give each one its proper due.

Yet it is important for us, in our study together, to put these God-given provisions into perspective. Then we will see more clearly God's "eternal power and divine nature" (Rom 1:20). And through our study we will be able to pour more meaning into our singing of the doxology: "Praise God, all creatures here below!"

Most of us have had awesome experiences in God's creation. Perhaps we have stood at the edge of a great canyon, or at the feet of giant trees in an ancient forest, or in the center of a great storm, or in a flowering meadow as the morning dew lifted quietly. And perhaps this experience has made us want to sing, "How Great Thou Art"! How I wish I could walk with you now to a place that would bring forth that song, for that would put you into the right frame of mind for what you are about to read. Open your mind now to the awesome wonder of our Lord's creation!

Seven Provisions of the Creator

In the remainder of this chapter I will identify seven of God's magnificent provisions for creation. These seven provisions—many of which are celebrated in Psalm 104—are indicative of the remarkable integrity and beauty that have engendered awe, wonder, and respect for the Creator and for creation through the ages.

Energy Exchange

Our star, the sun, pours forth immense energy in all directions. Whatever object lies in the path of its rays is heated. A very small part of the sun's immense radiated energy is intercepted by our tiny planet earth, 93 million miles distant from this star. This small amount energizes everything on earth—all of life, ocean currents, and the winds and storms.

But this energy tends to heat the earth, and it is necessary that this immense energy input be balanced by earth itself radiating energy back into space at the same rate that it is being received, on average. If more energy comes to earth than leaves, earth warms up. If more energy is radiated back into space than comes in, earth cools down.

And it is here that the thin layer of gases that envelop this planet serve a very important function. This layer is composed of water vapor, carbon dioxide, and other gases that trap and delay some of the sun's energy, slowing the re-radiation of the sun's energy back into outer space. As a result, Earth becomes warm—but not *too* warm. It is largely the provision of these specific gases—in just the right amounts—that make Earth's temperatures warm enough to support the wondrous fabric of life we call the biosphere.

Our atmosphere works very much like the glass of a greenhouse that lets sunlight in but makes it difficult for the heat to get out. We experience this "greenhouse effect" on the sunny side of our houses and in our cars when they're parked in sunlight on cold winter days.

This greenhouse effect is one of God's very important provisions for creation. It makes earth warm and habitable for all of God's creatures. If David or another biblical psalmist would have known of greenhouse gases, we likely would have a psalm in our Bible that praised God for such a provision. It may have sounded like this:

You energize earth with an outpouring of light;
  you bathe it with empowering rays.
You keep earth warm as with a blanket;
  you keep its heat near your creatures' hearts.
Your biosphere flourishes;
  the earth is full of your creatures.

But there is a dangerous side to the sun's energy. Beyond what can be seen by our eyes, beyond the blue and violet end of the spectrum, lies dangerous—even deadly—ultraviolet radiation.

Not only does the sun make living and nonliving things warm up, but it also conveys high energy levels that break chemical bonds, break molecules apart, and disrupt and destroy living tissues. Of special concern is the breaking of DNA—the genetic blueprint chemical of all living things. The destruction of DNA kills microscopic creatures and induces skin cancer in us and other living organisms.

But here we find another of the Creator's remarkable provisions. In the gaseous envelope of earth high in the atmosphere is a gas that absorbs ultraviolet light. That gas is ozone, and all of it together makes up what we call the "ozone layer" or "ozone shield." If one were to collect all this gas and place it at sea level atmospheric pressure and 32 degrees Fahrenheit, it would be only enough to make an envelope about one-eighth of an inch thick around the earth! And yet, that amount of ozone is enough to prevent most of the sun's ultraviolet radiation from penetrating our atmosphere and entering the household of life. That's why God's creatures are able to inhabit the earth.

If the biblical psalmist would have known of this provision by the Creator, perhaps we would have had this verse in one of the psalms:

The creatures that dwell in the shelter of God's providence
*   rest in the shadow of the Almighty.*
God covers the earth with a protective shield;
*   God guards the life he has made to inhabit earth.*
How great are your provisions O Lord!
You so love your world that you protect its life!

Soil Building

Those of us who garden know that composting and spading plants back into the soil makes the soil better and richer. This process, called "cycling," also takes place naturally as the earth's soil is renewed.

Soil gets richer and more supportive of life as it responds through time to climate, rainfall, and the organisms that live in it. Various remarkable cycles are involved in this development: the carbon cycle, the water cycle, the nitrogen cycle . . . and on it goes. These various cycles produce a veritable symphony of processes that allow bare landscapes—even bare rock—eventually to support a rich and diverse fabric of living things.

Soil-building teaches patience. It takes about one hundred years to produce one half-inch of topsoil. And that's the highest rate—sometimes only one-eighth of an inch of soil is produced in a century! The dynamic fabric of roots, soil organisms, and soils that bind together the surface of this biosphere makes one stand in awe of God's patience as Provider. For "with the Lord a day is like a thousand years, and a thousand years is like a day" (2 Pet. 3:8).

Where does this soil building happen? Everywhere! In the cool of the temperate zones, this soil building produces our prairie and woodland soils. Farther toward Earth's poles it produces the soils of our northern forests. And in the tropics it produces the reddish soils. In every part of the world the land is nurtured, refreshed, and renewed.

The cycling of Earth's materials and soil building help hold the whole world together. These processes support creation's integrity. They help renew the face of the earth. If hymnbook editors were looking for appropriate music to reflect this gift from God, they might well commission a canon in which recycling notes and interweaving themes would remind us of God's cyclical provisions. If in 1923 Thomas Chisholm had wanted to include this idea in his famous hymn about God's faithfulness, he might have written something like this:

Summer and winter and springtime and harvest,
sun, moon, and stars in their courses above,
join with all nature in manifold witness
to thy great faithfulness, mercy, and love.

Air and all elements, marvelously cycling,
tuned to the will of thy most loving grace,
building earth's soil and supporting thy creatures
steeped in thy love across earth's wondrous face.

Cycling

Recycling is not a recent invention. It is part and parcel of the way the world works. The whole creation uses, reuses, and uses again the various substances contained in the soil, water, and air for maintaining its living and non-living fabric.

1. Carbon Cycle

Carbon is the basic raw material from which the carbon-based stuff of life is made. And even as you sit reading this book, you're contributing to the process of recycling this commodity. As every living thing—whether human, raccoon, lizard, or gnat—breathes out, carbon dioxide enters the atmosphere. This carbon-stuff is transferred to the animals and microscopic life that depend upon it for food. And, sooner or later, these consuming creatures return the carbon back to the atmosphere as they breathe out carbon dioxide or as they die and decay.

2. Hydrologic Cycle

Water too is cycled and recycled—and in more ways than just by our water-treatment facilities:

- Taken up in the bodies of animals, it is released from those bodies through breathing, sweating, panting, and ridding of wastes. In this way, water finds its way back into the atmosphere.

- Taken up by the roots of plants, water is pumped right up through the bundles of tubing in the roots, stems, and leaves of plants and back to the atmosphere. Some is used together with carbon dioxide to produce the stuff of life that, after use by plants and animals as a building material and fuel, is once again released to the atmosphere.

- The water that is released from living organisms joins water that has evaporated from lakes, streams, soil, and other surfaces. This water eventually forms the rain, sleet, or snow that again waters the face of earth. Some water seeps through the soil back to the roots of plants; some water slips past these roots to enter the groundwater to be pumped through wells for human use or to emerge as springs; some water runs off to streams and other surface waters again to evaporate to reform the clouds from whence it came.

As water is evaporated or transpired to the air, most of the impurities it contained are left behind. This sweet distillation process expresses God's bountiful love for the world. And the clouds, great condensations of distilled watery vapors, rain this symbol of God's love down again to water the earth.

Thy bountiful care, what tongue can recite?
It breathes in the air, it shines in the light;
it streams from the hills, it descends to the plain,
and sweetly distills in the dew and the rain.

O worship the King, all glorious above,
O gratefully sing his power and his love.
Your ransomed creation, with glory ablaze,
in true adoration shall sing to your praise!

This beautiful hymn reflects the declaration of Psalm 104, which testifies:

He makes springs pour water into the ravines;
  it flows between the mountains.
They give water to all the beasts of the field;
  the wild donkeys quench their thirst.
The birds of the air nest by the waters;
  they sing among the branches.
He waters the mountains from his upper chambers;
  the earth is satisfied by the fruit of his work.

—Psalm 104:10-13

Cycles upon cycles . . . cycles within cycles . . . cycles of cycles . . . the creation is permeated with cycles. Each of these is empowered by energy poured out from the sun; each is empowered by God's grace poured out through his Son.

Earth's natural communities rely upon all of this cycling in creation. The biosphere—that great big envelope of life that covers the face of the earth—is what we and all God's creatures inhabit. And it is comprised of prairies, oceans, forests, lakes, glades, woodlands, brooks, and marshes. In other words, it is comprised of ecosystems.

Waubesa Marsh, the big wetland on which I live, is one of these ecosystems. Like every other ecosystem on earth, the marsh has its animals, plants, soils, and climate:

- the sandhill cranes whose six-feet wingspans, 70-year life spans, and bugling calls seemingly command the great marsh;

- the iron bacteria whose tiny size and very short lives would escape our notice except for the oil-like film they create over the quiet waters;

- the deep peat soil at the lake's edge that extends to a dizzying depth of 95 feet and holds within itself a record of pollens, seeds, and other remains that define its long history;

- the ebb and flow of water that comes in from flowing springs and falling rain and leaves by evaporation and by transpiration through the pores of wetland plants.

These creatures and their interactions, and much more, make up the wetland ecosystem.

Ecosystems are places of immense ecological harmony. Not every creature plays the same tune, but in many ways they are all in tune with each other. A great marsh may seem unstructured and disordered, but it is actually a highly ordered system in which each creature interacts with the other creatures to form an integrated whole. And what is true of wetlands is also true of forests, prairies, lakes, and deserts. Each is a kind of symphony.

The biosphere is a symphony of symphonies. The creatures that inhabit earth's ecosystems maintain and sustain the living fabric of the biosphere—as they reproduce, they continue to bring forth life from death. Through this process they cycle and recycle the basic stuff of creation, all powered by the sun. And over all this activity, God provides everything these creatures need to continue through the years and generations. In 1949, Stuart Hine responded to all of this wonderful harmony by writing the following:

O Lord my God, when I in awesome wonder
consider all the works thy hand hath made . . .

When through the woods and forest glades I wander,
I hear the birds sing sweetly in the trees;
when I look down from lofty mountain grandeur
and hear the brook and feel the gentle breeze;

Then sings my soul, my Savior God, to thee:
how great thou art,
how great thou art!

Water Purification

Taking a cue from nature, many water-treatment plants in our cities purify water by filtering it through beds of sand in a process called *percolation*. Water that percolates naturally through the soil is purified in the same way, but usually over much greater distances through soil and rock. By the time we pull up the groundwater to our homes from our wells it is usually fit to drink. This same purified water eventually supplies the flowing springs that feed the wetlands, lakes, and ravines.

You also know that purified water is returned to the air by evaporation from the surfaces of water, land, and organisms, and from transpiration through the pores of leaves. We call this process *evapotranspiration*, or simply *ET*.

Moving waters also serve as natural water purifiers. Normal levels of waste in natural ecosystems are cleaned up by brooks, streams, and rivers. By the time water moves a few miles downstream, the waste products and impurities that were put in upstream are largely removed.

Finally, the great marsh where I reside and other wetlands across the globe serve as water purifiers under natural conditions. When water containing eroded soil enters a wetlands area, the soil particles are filtered out. In many instances, dissolved chemicals also are removed from the water by wetland plants. Through this process wetland waters are cleaned up before they enter rivers and lakes, which makes these bodies of water habitable for other life.

Your spirit, O Lord, makes life to abound.
The earth is renewed, and fruitful the ground . . .

God causes the springs of water to flow
in streams from the hills to valleys below.
The Lord gives the streams for all living things there,
while birds with their singing enrapture the air.
Down mountains and hills your showers are sent.
With fruit of your work the earth is content.

Creative Fruitfulness

The whole creation is blessed with fruitfulness and abundant life. The home we call the biosphere is woven into a beautiful fabric of life that envelops earth. Through its intricately interwoven threads, this fabric tells the story of the household of life.

Take, for instance, flowering plants, of which there are 250,000 species: orchids, grasses, daisies, maples, sedges, lilies; all in amazingly colorful abundance and beauty. And each of these interrelates in its own distinctive way with water, soil, air, and numerous other kinds of organisms throughout its life span. Beyond these there are another quarter million species of other kinds of plants, and more beyond that. And these are not merely scattered—each species is situated in intricate dynamic relationships with the rest of the species with whom they interrelate.

When I was in ninth grade, I recall learning that there were a total of 1 million different kinds of living creatures. By the time I was in graduate school, I remember learning that there were 5 million species. Today we believe there are between 5 million and 40 million species of living things on our earth! The biodiversity of earth is so great that we realize that we are just now beginning to name the creatures. Thus far we have named only about 1.5 million of these species.

It is difficult to convey my own utter amazement at the seemingly infinite variety of life on earth. I'm even more amazed that, despite the dangers nearly every species faces as it goes through its life cycle, most species persist generation after generation, reproducing after their kind. Even though climates, landscapes, and other environmental factors shift continually, each species persists because each is endowed with the capacity to adapt to changing conditions. Each generation has its own variety—hardly any two offspring are exactly alike. Such variety produces individuals who will be able to adapt to new and unanticipated changes in the environment. God not only provides for the continuance of each species but also enables each to adapt to new situations. Therefore life doesn't merely persist—it flourishes.

Once again we can turn to the psalmist to lead us in praise:

How many are your works, O LORD!
In wisdom you made them all;
the earth is full of your creatures.
There is the sea, vast and spacious,
teaming with creatures beyond number—
living things both large and small.

—Psalm 104:24-25

I remember vividly the reading of Genesis 1 given by Atibisi, an African palynologist (palynology is the study of pollen and spores). She sat on the floor with the rest of us scientists and theologians in our Malaysian meeting room prior to our deliberations on the status of God's creation and our stewardship. She recited this passage with awesome wonder and God-praising joy, using pollen profiles that unraveled the records of peat soil deposits extending back to the earliest days of African agriculture. At the conclusion of her reading this doctor proclaimed, "This is so true; never has there been written a more beautiful and truthful account of the coming of the biological diversity of our Lord's earth. 'God said, "Let the waters bring forth swarms of living creatures, and birds that fly above the earth across the expanse of the sky." And the Lord blessed them and said, "Be fruitful and increase in number and fill the water in the seas, and let the birds increase on the earth. . . ." ' "

Only a knowledgeable biological scientist who deals with the life of the distant past and who is also an African storyteller could "tell it like it is" in this way. God causes the waters to bring forth swarms of creatures, and creation is blessed with fruitfulness. And God's blessing is everywhere evident, awesome, and wondrous!

Global Circulations of Water and Air

Because of its $23\frac{1}{2}$-degree tilt, our earth gets unequally heated from season to season. The northern hemisphere gets far more solar radiation in the northern summer than in winter. The opposite is true of the southern hemisphere. The earth's daily rotation also contributes to this unequal heat distribution.

These seasonal and daily temperature differences drive the flows of water and air from place to place. The heat flow is constrained by land masses and mountain ranges. These are the basic principles behind earth's atmospheric and oceanic circulations.

As water and air circulate around the globe, they move about many different materials such as carbon dioxide produced by animal and plant respiration, oxygen produced by photosynthesis, and water vapor in the form of rain, sleet, or snow. Global circulations are in a very real way the ventilation system of the biosphere. They provide the "breath" of life on a planetary scale and serve a vital function as they water all of the living things that cover the earth.

If David or another biblical psalmist would have known of these wondrous global circulations and of the way they spread water vapor and gases that are vital to life on earth, we might have had a psalm in our Bible that went something like this:

> You refresh the creatures with vital breath;
> 	you bathe your works in winds of life.
> Your providence is sure.
> Pastures green breathe life to flocks;
> 	to which your sheep return their breath.
> Creation is secure.
> You ventilate the land, and aerate your creatures.
> 	Your blowing renews the face of the earth.

Human Ability to Learn from Creation

God created human beings with the ability to learn from creation. We have the ability to probe and investigate God's world, to record in our mind's eye what we see, feel, hear, and smell. We have minds that create images of our world; images that help us when we plan and do our work in the world. These images—of our hometown, our family, the great expanse of a forest or marsh, or the tiny life we observed under a microscope—are continually tested against our experience. We learn from our mistakes, we learn from others whose observations and experiments we trust, and we revise our models of the world so that they better represent the world in which we live.

This ability to learn from what creation teaches us comes from God. A 1975 study of Hanunoo tribe of the Philippine Islands, for example, found that an average adult from the tribe could identify 1,600 different species—all without the help of modern science. The study showed that these people had learned some 400 more plant species than previously recorded in a modern systematic botanical survey. What's more, these people also knew how these plants could be used for food, construction, crafts, and medicine. And they knew where to find all of them—they knew their homes and habitats, their "ecology." Studies have produced similar findings in other areas of the world, such as Nigeria.[2]

[2]Awa, N. "Participation and Indigenous Knowledge in Rural Development." *Knowledge* 10:304-316, 1989.

This ability to build mental models of all aspects of creation—from plants and atoms to home and cosmos—is essential for meaningful human life. These scientific models are nurtured and often refined by our human culture, which is also a gift from God. Early on we learned the warmth of our mother's love; in the days of our youth we were imbued with love for our Creator through our parents and churches; and in our vocations we daily learn from the people and writings that touch us.

But we also have the ability to work with the information that we receive. When presented with concrete evidence or convincing arguments, we might even "change our minds" about a particular issue. By God's providence, we have minds that have the ability to think and reason. By God's providence, these minds are informed, cultured, and cultivated by God's world and God's Word.

Christian people are "re-minded" by God's Word that the earth is the Lord's and everything in it. God is the one who made all things, holds all things together, and reconciles all things to himself (cf. John 1, Col. 1). More than that, we are encouraged to be like-minded with Jesus Christ, the One who created, sustains, and reconciles the creation. Learning to adopt the mind of Christ is a task that lasts a lifetime. The Christian culture with which we are infused prays:

May the mind of Christ, my Savior,
live in me from day to day,
by his love and power controlling
all I do or say.

What does it mean to have the mind of Jesus Christ, the one of whom it is written:

He is the image of the invisible God, the firstborn over all creation.
For by him all things were created: things in heaven and on earth,
visible and invisible, whether thrones or powers or rulers or au-
thorities; all things were created by him and for him. He is before
all things, and in him all things hold together. And he is the head
of the body, the church; he is the beginning and the firstborn from
among the dead, so that in everything he might have the su-
premacy. For God was pleased to have all his fullness dwell in
him, and through him to reconcile to himself all things, whether
things on earth or things in heaven, by making peace through his
blood, shed on the cross.

—*Colossians 1:15-20*

The Creator, in providing for us and all people, has given us minds and nurturing cultures that allow us to imagine and know how the world works. We human beings have been granted the ability to know creation and to act upon that knowledge. This provision allows Jesus' followers to adopt the mind of Christ. This means that those who follow Jesus not only learn from creation but also engage in its care, keeping, and reconciliation in accord with God's love for the world.

Suggestions for Group Session

Getting Started

The busy pace of modern life easily distracts us from looking closely at the way God provides for us. The air we breathe, the rain that waters the land, the new life that breaks forth from tiny seeds—sometimes we simply take these amazing gifts for granted. We might never take the time to think of the wheat plants whose fruit we eat every day, or of the remarkable beauty of the leaves we enjoy in our salads, or of why we never have to rake the leaves that fall in the forest. The greatest gifts of creation are free. God pours these gifts out to each one of us, every single day. This chapter celebrates these gifts.

As a group meeting for the first time, begin by each mentioning some part of God's creation for which you are especially thankful. If you wish, describe a recent experience in which you've particularly enjoyed some aspect of creation.

Then together read the words from "Our World Belongs to God," the Contemporary Testimony of the Christian Reformed Church:

> God formed the land, the sky, and the seas,
> making the earth a fitting home
> for the plants, animals,
> and humans he created.
> The world was filled with color, beauty, and variety;
> it provided room for
> work and play,
> worship and service,
> love and laughter.

Join together in prayer, thanking God for these and other provisions in creation. Conclude your prayer time with praise to God for Jesus Christ as the one through whom the world was made, is held together, and is reconciled to its Creator (cf. John 1 and Col. 1).

Group Discussion and Activity

Following are suggestions for a variety of activities that you can do in your group. It's likely that you won't have time to do them all, so please choose the questions and activities that you think are most appropriate.

From Chapter One

1. This chapter describes seven provisions that God has established for creation. Which one impressed you the most? Which one was new to you? What do these provisions—and any others that you can think of—tell you about God?

From Your Experience

1. Take a sheet of newsprint and as a group make a list of different ways that God shows love to the world. Think of the teachings of both the Old and New Testaments, and think of the evidence of God's love for the world that we see in creation. Confine your list to the left half of the newsprint sheet.

2. On the right side of the newsprint, write the group's ideas on how we can image God's love for the world. As Christians who are charged with caring for God's creation, what specifically might we do to act on that obligation?

3. Read the following material written by Abraham Kuyper, a prominent Reformed theologian and author who once was prime minister of the Netherlands.

> *God loves the world.*
>
> *Of course not in its sinful strivings. . . . But God loves the world for the sake of its origin; because God has thought it out; because God has created it; because God has maintained it and maintains it to this day.*
>
> *Not we have made the world, and thus in our sin we have not maltreated an art product of our own. No, that world was the contrivance, the work, and the creation of the Lord our God. It was and is His world, which belonged to Him, which He had created for His glory, and for which we with that world were by Him appointed. Not to us did it belong, but to Him. It was His. And His divine world we have spoiled and corrupted.*
>
> *And herein roots the love of God, that He will repair and renew this world, His own creation, His own work of wisdom, His own work of art, which we have upset and broken, and polish it again to new lustre. . . .*
>
> *And therefore whoever would be saved with that world, as God loves it, let him accept the Son, Whom God has given to that world, in order to save the world. Let him not continue stand-*

*ing afar off, let him not hesitate, but flee to God's cities of refuge
. . . where God has revealed His impenetrable compassions.*

—Reprinted in translation in 1928 as a chapter entitled
"So God Loved the World!" in *Keep Thy Solemn Feasts:
Meditations by Abraham Kuyper,* Grand Rapids, Michigan:
Wm. B. Eerdmans Publishing Company, pp. 70-71.

1. How does Kuyper show that he has a biblical understanding of the world?

2. Describe in your own words what Kuyper is saying about creation, human beings, and the Savior.

From the Bible

1. Read Psalm 19. What does this psalm say about God's role in creation?

2. Read Romans 1:20. What does this verse have to say about God's self-revelation in nature?

3. What does Colossians 1:16-17 say about God's continuing care for his creation?

Closing Prayer

Enter into prayer as a group, with various members contributing their thanks for God's love for the world. Conclude the prayer by thanking God for sending Jesus, God's one and only Son, so that we and all things could be reconciled to him.

TWO

SEVEN DEGRADATIONS OF CREATION[1]

Introduction

There was a time when I was oblivious to human abuse of creation. Snakes were always to be found under the tar paper and discarded sheet metal in the dump at the edge of town, and bullfrogs and bitterns were always to be found in the swamps of Reeds Lake. I guess I just thought, as I'm sure you also did in your youth, that the world had somehow always been this way.

It was years later, as I was doing my graduate work with my wife, Ruth, on the desert of southern California, that I first became powerfully aware of the way human beings were abusing creation. It was then I learned about the foolishness of our species. People were coming to build homes in the very place where I was studying the desert iguana, a then-abundant, large white lizard that lived in the dry and thirsty land at the mouth of Deep Canyon.

There at the foot of the San Jacinto Mountains workers came with sprinklers to wet the desert surface so it could be shaped with a blade, covered with a slab of concrete, and finished with a house. They were building here and there on a great, gently sloping triangle of land, directing picture windows of air-conditioned living rooms downslope to capture the magnificent view of the desert's grand sweep across the Coachella Valley.

---

[1] A full treatment of the provisions of the biosphere, in addition to a description of environmental abuses and needed responses, can be found in *Environmental Science: The Way the World Works* by Bernard J. Nebel and Richard T. Wright (Englewood Cliffs, NJ: Prentice-Hall, 1993).

What had formed this great triangle of land that looked so much like a river delta? The year Ruth and I were there, it had rained only two and fifty-four hundredths of an inch—normal for this dry and thirsty land—so it clearly couldn't have been a river delta. Or could it?

An old prospector who had wandered that desert for decades looking for gold explained: "Nope, it mainly never rains here. But, when it does, watch out!" Pointing to the heights of the mountains that towered over the desert beyond a widely yawning canyon, he said, "Why, once a lifetime or so, up high in them mountains, it thunders and lightnin's, it rains cats and dogs. . . . Floods race down this canyon spitting sand, rocks, and boulders onto the desert. That's what makes this delta here. Even boulders the size of houses come rollin' down that delta in the ragin' river." He then lowered his arm and, pointing to a protected point near the edge of the canyon he said, "Over there, outside the path of the canyon's once-a-century fury, is where the native people camped. They knew what this great river delta meant!"

The developers must have overlooked that native wisdom. For as we studied desert lizards, roads for a city were being planned on that delta. Before long, Palm Desert, California, stood right in the mouth of a giant river that once a century or so could roll rocks the size of houses onto them from the canyon above!

Upon traveling back to the area, I discovered that what used to be my study site is now the approach pad to a drive-in bank. What's more, the new owners of the old "Gates of the Desert Lodge," which sits right in the heart of the habitat of these once-abundant lizards, looked bewildered when I asked them about the desert iguana. With puzzled expressions and bothered disbelief they replied to what they deemed complete non-sense by saying, "Lizards?"

For now, you see, I was standing in the city. The home of the hundred or so big white lizards that I studied was covered with a drive-in bank, and that was surrounded by a city. Nearby, cattails grew in a roadside ditch—wetland creatures that were thriving here in runoff from overwatered lawns. I did find one big white lizard. It was in the local zoo. Whether they knew it or not, all the people living on this great river delta at the mouth of Deep Canyon were waiting for a great flood.

No longer am I ignorant about what people are doing in and to God's creation. And while I still sing, "Praise God, all creatures here below," it has become more of a hopeful song. I sing hoping that the people who choose to build their homes in the mouths of desert streams, in the floodplains of great rivers, on earthquake faults, at the feet of volcanoes, on slippery un-stable slopes, or on drifting sands will blame themselves and not God when disaster strikes.

What is the status of creation today? How are we faring as stewards of God's world? This is a most important question to ask, for we have been entrusted with and given dominion over creation by God. How, we inquire, has the earth fared under our stewardship?

That's not an easy question to answer. But answering this question has been part of my professional work for a long time now. To the best of my ability I have done a computer search of 700,000 titles of articles on the environment. I have pruned this collection down to those written in the professional, refereed literature, and have organized these into major topics that I call "Seven Degradations of Creation."

Before I give this summary, however, I must say what I mean by "refereed literature." Without knowing the meaning of this term we will drift in a sea of undisciplined chatter and opinion, the talk of the town that frequently capsizes our efforts to discover what really is happening to "the environment."

We know how referees are used in sports—they make sure the game is played by the rules, calling "foul" when it's foul and "fair" when it's fair. Similarly, refereed literature also uses referees, people who read articles before they are published. When these referees cry "foul," the article they are reviewing never sees the light of day. "Strike one" means that the author is given one or two more chances to get things right—hopefully to "make a hit." Referees, both in professional publications and in sports, are carefully chosen for the depth and breadth of their knowledge, for their discernment and judgment, for their record of fairness, and for being free from the influence of the sponsors and spectators.

The editors of refereed or "primary" literature normally use three referees to critically evaluate each article or "paper" (as professional articles usually are called). After reading the article the referees make an independent and anonymous report, suggesting that the editor either reject, publish, or publish the article with revisions. If the editor gets a mixed review, the paper may be sent to still more highly qualified referees. If the paper must be revised, each revision is again reviewed by three referees. Articles that pass these reviews are published periodically in professional journals, usually by a professional society to whom the editor is responsible. This extremely disciplined procedure is employed to keep us researchers honest about what we know and what we do not know.

I have used such primary literature as the source of information in this chapter. But there are two more kinds of literature involved in environmental research. These are called "gray" and "popular" literature.

"Gray" literature consists of reports from government agencies such as the Environmental Protection Agency and the Department of Natural Resources, from colleges and universities, from granting agencies, and from institutes and foundations. This literature too is important, but it is not considered as authoritative since it does not undergo the same kind of disciplined review as does primary literature. Gray literature often uses different standards and is more susceptible to outside influences. Therefore it generally is not relied upon by professional researchers to give a basic understanding of how the world works and what is happening to it.

"Popular" literature is comprised of newspapers, magazines, leaflets and brochures. Like gray literature, it also is important, but it is not normally considered authoritative.

What I present here as "Seven Degradations of Creation" is based upon primary or refereed literature. That means I have not obtained my information from government or university reports, newspapers, opinion polls, television talk shows, or popular articles. Perhaps what I write about the degradations of creation may be less dramatic than what one can read or hear elsewhere; but it will not be boring. On the contrary, we will find that the magnitude of environmental abuse is overwhelming! So let us begin.

Seven Degradations of Creation

Land Conversion and Habitat Destruction

The earth's total land mass consists of 16,000 million acres that support some kind of vegetation and a nearly equal area of ice, snow, and rock. Current world cropland consists of 3,600 million acres. Since 1850, people have converted some 2,200 million acres of natural lands to human uses. This land conversion goes by different names, depending on what is done: it may be called "deforestation" (forests), "drainage" or "reclamation" (wetlands), "irrigation" (arid and semi-arid ecosystems), or "opening" (grasslands and prairies). The greatest land conversion underway today is tropical deforestation, which removes about 25 million acres of primary forest each year—an area the size of the state of Indiana.

The immensity of this destruction illustrates humanity's power to alter the face of earth. Why do we continue with tropical deforestation? Largely because we are *able* to do it. By clearing tropical forests we are able to enjoy inexpensive items like plywood, bathroom tissue, hamburger meat, and orange juice, among other things. All this comes at the cost of destroying the long-term sustainability of soils, forest creatures, and resident people.

In the United States, the remaining woodlots and the habitats they provide are replaced with parking lots, buildings, and additions to homes, offices, and churches. In the United States, about 3 million of the 400 million acres of cropland that is used for agriculture is converted to urban uses every year. In Canada and the U.S., fields for grazing and crops are no longer "carved" from forests; they *replace* the forests. And houses are replacing some of the best cropland.

The Bible has a verse that speaks to this particular abuse of creation: "Woe to you who add house to house and join field to field till no space is left and you live alone in the land" (Isa. 5:8).

Species Extinctions

Every single day, more than three species of plants and animals are extinguished. Their kind, their lineage, is cut off from the face of the earth forever. If we have the 40 million species of plants and animals that some scientists estimate we have on earth, then that rate may be eight times higher.

While we have given names to most species of plants and animals in North America and Europe, we have not named most tropical species. Yet, named or not, they appear in our stores, lumber yards, offices, boats, and homes as cheap plywood, furniture, and lizard-skin wallets and shoes. Children around the world are paid pennies to bring in skins of once-living creatures, turning them in to be manufactured into items that will soon become the latest fashion statement.

We add to this species destruction when we destroy natural habitats by expanding our homes and churches, eliminating woodlots on our farms, and removing the vegetation that once separated fields. Even butterflies, once so common in the everyday life of city and country, are losing hold as their habitats are destroyed, their food plants are killed by herbicides, and they themselves are killed by widespread use of "broad-spectrum" pesticides. Some individuals now urge us to plant butterfly gardens as natural "arks" for preserving these creatures who otherwise might perish. Others urge us to preserve remnant woodlots and prairies as natural "arks" in response to what has become a "deluge of people." Even now the church-yards of England are the sole remaining habitats for some creatures.

A verse to ponder as we consider these losses is Genesis 6:19: "You are to bring into the ark two of all living creatures," says the Creator to Noah, "male and female, to keep them alive with you. . . ."

Land Abuse

What once was the tall grass prairie is what we now call the "corn belt," the region where we now grow that tall grass whose ears feed us, our hogs, and our cattle. In much of this tall grass prairie, two bushels of top-soil are lost for every bushel of corn produced.

Contributing heavily to land abuse is the widespread use of manufactured chemicals. The use of pesticides and herbicides proliferated after military chemists turned their efforts toward developing "peaceful" uses of biocides after World War II. These chemicals made it possible for farmers to plant any crop year after year on the same land—which they did, often at the urging of chemical manufacturers and salespeople. Crop rotation from corn to soy beans to alfalfa hay to pastures was abandoned. Farm animals were kept in feedlots, which freed up confinements and fenced-in areas for more intensified use of the land. Whatever topsoil was lost by the resulting wind and water erosion was compensated for by increasing fertilizer inputs. What *could have* been done *has been* done, and the soil life has been devastated.

Earthworms no longer inhabit most farmlands. The microscopic life of the soil has been severely altered. Most of the land never rests. Birds no longer live in the fencerows and hedgerows that once separated the fields. The creatures that once thrived on the prairies, grasslands, forests, and fields have been driven off as their habitats have become chemical deserts. Even many domestic creatures are deprived both of pasture and pastor.

As we consider this abuse, we might reflect on the meaning of this verse from the Bible: "When you enter the land I am going to give you," commands the Torah, "the land itself must observe a Sabbath to the LORD . . ." (Lev. 25:1). God warned Moses that if the people did not obey this law, the land would be laid waste. After the land had become a desert, the people would be driven away. Then the land would have the rest it did not have during the Sabbaths that the people lived on it (Lev. 26:14, 32, 35).

Resource Conversion and Wastes and Hazards Production

Human ingenuity has created some 70,000 different chemicals, about 10,000 of which are part of the environment in which we live and breathe. Yet living organisms have had no experience with these materials. Unlike chemicals made by organisms and by the earth, some of these chemicals leave living things defenseless. Among them are many specifically designed to destroy life: biocides, pesticides, herbicides, avicides, and fungicides are literally life-killers, pest-killers, herb-killers, bird-killers, and fungus-killers. Other materials, such as petroleum, pose additional problems for living organisms. Oil spills destroy life and habitats and devastate human livelihoods on shores and seas.

Every item in our homes, offices, churches, and industries is a reworked part of creation. Every product we make, each housing and commercial development we build, every road we travel alters creation. While knowing this full well, we neglect to recognize the immense changes that 5.6 billion of us bring to the earth. We remove parts of the creation, make products and by-products, and produce discards and wastes.

Consider styrofoam cups as an example. We move oil by ship from Saudi Arabia to chemical plants. There the oil is transformed into *monomers*, which are then transported to factories that transform them into styrofoam cups. These styrofoam cups are distributed to stores and then to churches for after-service coffee. They are discarded in wastebaskets, moved to trash containers, and trucked to landfills. As the cups decompose, some of their remains enter groundwater in the form of leachate that may contaminate springs and wells; other remains enter the atmosphere as carbon dioxide, methane, and (until recently) chloroflourocarbons (CFC's), which alter the earth's energy exchange with the sun.

At the base of our abuse of creation is a fundamental difference in human and natural economies. Ours is mainly a flow-through economy. Our "economy" taps creation's wealth at one point and discards its by-products at another. Nature's economy is cyclical. Ecosystems sustain themselves by cycling materials. And creation's economy is threatened by our own. We interfere with its cycles on a grand scale as we "trash" its creatures, pollute its waters, and mow down its vegetation.

As we consider this abuse, we must thoughtfully consider this passage from Ezekiel: "Is it not enough for you to feed on the good pasture?" asks the sovereign Lord. "Must you also trample the rest . . . with your feet? Is it not enough for you to drink clear water? Must you also muddy the rest with your feet?" (Ezek. 34:18).

Global Toxification

We already noted in an earlier chapter how weather, oceans, and river systems transport and distribute materials around the globe. Of the thousands of chemical substances humans have created, hundreds have been injected into the atmosphere, discharged in rivers, and leaked into the groundwater. These substances join in the global circulation cycle. That's why DDT shows up in Antarctic penguins, and why biocides exist in a remote lake on Lake Superior's Isle Royale. Cancer has permeated some herring gull populations. Chemical and oil spills kill creation's life on a massive scale.

In the intercourse between creation's economy and ours, we perpetrate "the rape of the earth." No longer are only *local* environments affected by *local* polluters. Local pollution has global repercussions. Global toxification affects all life: all creatures, great and small; all people, rich and poor.

We need to reflect on the words of Jeremiah 2:7 when we consider what we have done to God's creation: "I brought you into a fertile land to eat its fruit and rich produce. But you came and defiled my land and made my inheritance detestable."

Alteration of Planetary Energy Exchange

Earth's temperature depends on the balance between energy received and energy reradiated into outer space. Carbon dioxide and some other 25 to 30 human-made chemicals act as "greenhouse gases"—they allow sunlight to penetrate the earth's atmosphere but intercept and absorb energy reradiated from the earth. Carbon dioxide and these human-made chemicals, including CFC's, operate like the glass of a greenhouse or the windshield of a closed automobile. As car windshields allow sunlight to flow into cars but prevent reradiated infrared radiation from flowing back, so these greenhouse gases trap heat.

With the right concentration of these gases, earth retains enough heat to maintain temperatures much as we have experienced them for centuries. But burning and exposing carbon-containing materials to oxygen brings rising concentrations of atmospheric carbon dioxide, allowing less heat to escape back to outer space. This activity contributes to global warming. The increase in atmospheric carbon dioxide comes from burning

33

petroleum, coal, and wood; from deforestation; and from draining wetlands. Adding to the effects of increasing carbon dioxide are other greenhouse gases produced by our chemical industry, such as CFC refrigerants in our air conditioners and refrigerators.

Earth's temperature has been rising very slowly over centuries as evidenced by melting snow caps, receding glaciers, and slowly rising sea level. But now, with our addition of greenhouse gases to the atmosphere, this rise will likely accelerate. This increase in greenhouse gases will have consequences not only for earth's temperature, but also for the *distribution* of temperature across the planet, with changes in patterns of rainfall and drought, and even—ironically—lower temperatures in some places in the world.

CFC's operate not only as greenhouse gases. They also destroy earth's ozone layer. This layer, located in the outer atmosphere, absorbs much of the sun's ultraviolet radiation, thereby protecting genetic material of living creatures from damage it would otherwise sustain from the radiation. The ozone layer's destruction results in more ultraviolet light reaching creatures on earth, us included, where this radiation causes, among other things, an increase in skin cancer.

One Old Testament writer asks, "Is this the way you repay the LORD, O foolish and unwise people? Is he not your father, your Creator, who made you and formed you?" (Deut. 32:6).

Human and Cultural Abuse

The Amish of Lancaster County, Pennsylvania, are threatened by a proposed highway through the center of their 300-year-old sustainable community. Other cultural pressures, such as increased land taxes and encroaching urban development, compel many Amish and Mennonite families and communities to abandon their farms. Likewise, in the tropics, longstanding cultures living cooperatively with the forest are being wiped off the land by force, death, and legal procedures devised to deprive them of their traditional lands. As these people are run off or extinguished, so is their rich, unwritten knowledge. The successful ways these people have had of living in harmony with the land are forgotten; names of otherwise undescribed forest creatures are lost; and information on the uses of a wide array of tropical species for human food, fiber, and medicine is wasted.

Both the great variety of natural species and the diversity of our agricultural heritage are being diminished. Seeds of a wide variety of plants suited to small farms and gardens are being displaced by new strains that are more suited to mechanized planting and harvesting. These new strains are uniform in color, size, and time of ripening. An aggressive economy, one that seeks to maximize immediate returns at the expense of long-term sustainability, is sweeping the globe.

Agri*culture* is being displaced by agri*business*. The meek people of the earth are being displaced by labor-saving technology. Powerless people are being pushed to the margins of the land or to the cities. Disconnected from the land that could have sustained them, they are driven into joblessness and poverty. In the name of conducting "good" business, finding "sound" investments, and making "good" money, powerful, wealthy individuals strip these powerless people of the ability to take care of themselves and the creation, depriving them of the inheritance of generations. These displaced persons in turn bring about a worldwide explosion of urban growth and a resulting cycle of poverty.

God's Word says, "Do not take advantage of each other. . . . The land must not be sold permanently, because the land is mine and you are but aliens and my tenants . . ." (Lev. 25:17, 23). The Bible also says that the land must be returned to the poor and the meek (Lev. 25:28). The Lord observes that "The stork in the sky knows her appointed seasons, and the dove, the swift and the thrush observe the time of their migration. But my people do not know the requirements of the LORD" (Jer. 8:7). In our modern age, we need to heed these long-standing words of instruction.

Choosing Life

Creation's garden abundantly yields blessed fruits, sustainably supporting us and all life in its God-declared goodness. We "disciples of the first Adam" have made the choice to extract more and yet more of the fruits of creation—even at the expense of destroying creation's protective provisions and blessed fruitfulness. Before this human onslaught fall the earth's creatures. Some have their populations severely depleted, while others are wiped off the face of the Creator's canvas. We have chosen to trash the great gallery of Earth's Maker, replacing it with our own creations. These new creations "are for the greatest good," surpass creation itself, and are "bigger than life." Under this arrogant assault on the fabric of the biosphere, "the earth dries up and withers. . . . The earth is defiled by its people" (Isa. 24:4-5).

Since the beginning of creation, we human beings have been making choices. Early on we made the choice to know good and evil. In the last several centuries we have chosen to take avarice and greed, those long-recognized vices, and redefine them as virtues. We have come to believe that "looking out for number one" means getting more and more for *me*. *Self*-interest, we now profess, is what brings the greatest good. Choices made for the creation, for the Creator, have been usurped by choices made for *me* and for "the economy." The world today professes, "Seek ye first a job, and all these other things will be added unto you."

God says through Moses, "I have set before you life and death, blessings and curses. Now choose life, so that you and your children may live and that you may love the LORD your God, listen to his voice, and hold fast to him" (Deut. 30:19-20).

Summing Up

Earth's crisis can best be summed up in these seven creation degradations:

1. The *alteration of earth's energy exchange* with the sun results in global warming and destruction of the earth's protective ozone shield.

2. *Land abuse* reduces available land for creatures and crops by "adding house to house and field to field" and destroys land by chemical overuse, erosion, and deforestation.

3. *Water-quality abuse* defiles groundwater, lakes, rivers, and oceans.

4. *Deforestation* each year removes as much primary forest acreage as the size of the state of Indiana and degrades an equal amount by overuse.

5. *Species extinction* finds more than three species of plants and animals eliminated from earth *each day*.

6. *Waste generation* and *global toxification* have far-reaching effects; they contaminate much more than just local environments.

7. *Human and cultural abuse* disregards long-standing knowledge of the land, discourages cooperation with creation, and decreases the number of garden varieties of food plants.

All of the above degradations are contrary to biblical teaching. While we are expected to enjoy the creation and its fruitfulness, we humans are not granted license to destroy the earth. While human beings are expected to be fruitful, so is the rest of creation: "Let the water teem with living creatures, and let birds fly above the earth across the expanse of the sky . . . . Be fruitful and increase in number and fill the water in the seas, and let the birds increase on the earth" (Gen. 1:20, 22).

Suggestions for Group Session

Getting Started

How easy it is to go about our busy lives without ever thinking about the consequences of our actions! We frequently "throw things away," never thinking about where "away" is. We spray a substance designed to kill an insect, never wondering whether that substance will kill or hurt other life as well. We decry the destruction of the great trees of California as we chat around our redwood picnic table. We are members of a society that has distanced itself from the results of its actions. And the result of all of this is that the environment is being abused. This chapter describes some of the major degradations of creation and helps build an understanding of why we need to be concerned for creation and for future generations.

Begin by reading together the following words from "Our World Belongs to God":

Sin is present everywhere—
in pride of race,
in arrogance of nations,
in abuse of the weak and helpless,
in disregard for water, air, and soil,
in destruction of living creatures. . . .

Open your session today with prayer. In your prayer time together, acknowledge God as the Creator and Ruler of the earth. Praise Jesus as the One through whom all things are made, are held together, and are reconciled. Confess that in our sinfulness we as human beings have abused creation. Ask God for forgiveness and for the grace to conduct reconciling works that are worthy of repentance.

Group Discussion and Activity

From Chapter Two

1. On the left side of a sheet of newsprint make a list of the seven degradations of creation noted in this chapter.

2. On the right side of the page write down how we personally contribute to each of these degradations in our daily lives.

From Your Experience

1. Think back to something that in your childhood or early youth was a wonderful part of creation, but that now has been abused or destroyed. Then share that memory with the members of the group.

2. Reread the segment about the styrofoam cup in the chapter. In a similar manner, identify one item that someone in the group has purchased in the last week and jot down on chalkboard or newsprint, in step-wise fashion, where the item originated, how it came eventually to you, and where it ultimately is going. Then discuss these questions:

   • How far will it have traveled when it reaches its final destination?

   • How much energy do you think was expended to make its journey possible?

   • What have been, what are, and what will be the impacts of its journey on creation's household of life?

3. What are the underlying causes of environmental abuse? To answer this question, each group member should jot down (on a notecard or separate sheet of paper) what he or she considers to be the greatest

environmental abuse we face in the world today. Then break into small groups of three or four and share what each person has written. Together decide what you believe to be the *underlying* cause or causes of all the degradations you have identified. Then report your conclusions to the entire group.

As a single, large group, pick one cause that was mentioned by all or most small groups. Discuss how we as individuals and as a body of believers can begin addressing this cause of environmental abuse.

4. Pick one of the seven degradations we have studied in this chapter and describe what we can do about it in our personal lives, church, and community.

From the Bible

1. Often the question is asked today, "Isn't it more important to save *people* than it is to save *species?*" Review the story of Noah recorded in Genesis 6 through 9, and decide, based upon that story, what the biblical answer might be to this question. If saving people was always more important than saving species, how might this story have been written?

2. Read Genesis 6:19, Isaiah 5:8, and Ezekiel 34:18. Explain what these passages have to say about God's intentions for us in regards to creation.

3. What does Leviticus 25:17, 23 say about our relationship to creation? Whose world is this, after all?

Closing Prayer

Consider what you have read and studied about the underlying cause or causes of environmental abuse. From all of this, think through the importance of confession and repentance. Conclude your session with a confessional prayer in which all members of the group are invited to participate.

THREE

CREATION'S CARE AND KEEPING: A BIBLICAL PERSPECTIVE

To stimulate thoughtful reflection in the second chapter, I embellished each of seven abuses of creation with a related verse or two from Scripture. I did not choose those verses as mere ornaments, but I did select them after I wrote the descriptions, and they were only more or less appropriate. Taking small bits of the Bible's wisdom and applying it to today is one way that we can use Scripture to gain insights into environmental and other issues. But the Bible can be applied to our lives in other, more powerful ways.

We know that over the centuries the Bible has been critically important to people who seek to live in love and obedience to God. The Bible's importance continues today, not only for church and home, but (and this surprises many Christians and non-Christians alike) also for the environment. The Bible is hardly a minor contributor when it comes to providing advice on caring for creation. In fact, the Bible provides such powerful environmental teachings that it can be thought of as a kind of ecological handbook on how to rightly live on earth!

Among its many teachings, the Bible helps us understand our privilege and our responsibility for environmental stewardship. It also helps us to address thoughtfully who we are, what we are prone to do, and the problems we create in creation.

The Bible's serious treatment of environmental matters should not surprise us. Since God created and sustains all of creation, we should expect the Bible to call us to bring honor to God. We should expect the Scriptures to support creation's proper care and keeping and to encourage us to maintain the integrity of the creation that, in the first chapter of Genesis, God repeatedly calls "good." Moreover, since the Bible professes Jesus Christ as the one through whom *all things* are reconciled, we certainly should expect the Bible to decry creation's destruction, to call for creation's restoration, and to look forward to the whole creation being made right again. And so it does!

Keeping in mind the abuses we have committed against creation and the need for restoration, it is helpful to read the Scriptures afresh, searching for their ecological insights on how we can rightly live on this planet. As we look into God's Word, I will identify seven biblical principles that help disclose the Bible's profound environmental message. No doubt you will be able to find many more.

Principle 1

As the Lord keeps and sustains us, so must we keep and sustain our Lord's creation.

Genesis 2:15 conveys a marvelous teaching. Here, God expects Adam to *serve* the garden and to *keep* it.

The Hebrew word for *serve ('abad)* is translated as *till, dress,* or *work* in most recent translations of the Bible. Adam and his descendants are expected to meet the needs of the garden so that it will persist and flourish. But how on earth can we *serve* creation? Shouldn't creation serve us instead?

When I discovered this translation of the word *'abad,* I called the library at Calvin College and Seminary to ask the reference librarian, Conrad Bult, if he could find any Bibles that translated this word as *serve.* Bult discovered, in *Young's Literal Translation of the Bible: A Revised Edition* (Grand Rapids, MI: Baker Book House, 1953), Genesis 2:15 translated in this way: "And Jehovah God taketh the man and causeth him to rest in the garden of Eden, to serve it and to keep it." What this means I will leave to you, my dear reader, as a puzzle that you can discuss with your friends.

God also expects us as Adam's descendants to *keep* the garden. This word *keep* is sometimes translated *tend, take care of, guard,* and *look after.* The Hebrew word upon which these translations of *keep* are based is the word *shamar.* And *shamar* indicates a loving, caring, sustaining type of keeping.

In our worship services, we often conclude with the Aaronic blessing from Numbers 6:24: "The LORD bless you and *keep* you." The word *keep* here is the same Hebrew word used in Genesis 2:15: *shamar.* When we invoke God's blessing to keep us, we are not asking that God keep us in a kind of preserved, inactive, uninteresting state. Instead we are calling on God to keep us in all of our vitality, with all of our energy and beauty. The keeping we expect of God when we invoke the Aaronic blessing is one that nurtures all of our life-sustaining and life-fulfilling relationships with our family members, with our neighbors and our friends, with the land, air, and water, and with our God. We ask God to love us, to care for us, and to sustain us in relationship to our natural and human environment.

So too with our keeping of God's creation. When we fulfill God's mandate that Adam and Eve *keep* the creation, we make sure that the creatures under our care and keeping are maintained in their proper, natural contexts. They must remain connected to members of the same species, to the many other species with which they interact, and to the soil, air, and water upon which they depend. The rich and full keeping that we invoke with the Aaronic blessing is the kind of rich and full keeping that we should bring to God's garden, to God's creatures, and to all of creation.

Principle 2
We must be disciples of Jesus Christ, the Creator, Sustainer, and Reconciler of all things.

No question about it—the Bible calls us to be disciples, or *followers after* someone. But we are not to be disciples of the first Adam who neglected to serve *('abad)* and to keep *(shamar)* the creation. He failed in his task of caring service and diligent keeping. We must not follow those like him who choose to go their own way and "do their own thing."

Instead, the Bible tells us, we must be disciples of the *last* Adam, Jesus Christ (1 Cor. 15:45). In John 3:16, the New Testament teaches that God loved the world so much that he gave his only Son to bring true life, to make things right again. "For as in Adam all die, so in Christ will all be made alive" (1 Cor. 15:20-22).

Those who follow the last Adam, Jesus Christ, follow the example of the one who makes all things new, the one who makes all things right again. Colossians 1:19-20 puts it this way: "For God was pleased to have all his fullness dwell in him, and through him to reconcile to himself *all things."*

Who is this Christ we are to follow? He is the One *by whom* all things were created (John 1). He is the One *for whom* all things were made (Col. 1). And he is the one *through whom* God redeems his people (Heb. 1).

God reaches out sacrificially to make things right again. Jesus Christ, the final Adam, undoes the damage done by the first Adam and his followers. While Adam's followers bring death and degradation, Christ brings life and restoration (Rom. 5:12ff). The children of God work as followers and disciples of the final Adam. People who are happy to be Christ's servant stewards are the people for whom the whole creation is eagerly looking.

We must, then, be disciples of Jesus Christ. We must walk in the footsteps of the One who reconciles all things. We must tread the path of the One who takes the form of a reconciling servant. We must be disciples of the last Adam, not of the first. We must work to reconcile all things to Christ.

Principle 3
We must provide for creation's sabbath rests.

In Exodus 20 and Deuteronomy 5, the Bible requires that one day in seven be set aside as a day of rest for people and animals. This sabbath day is given to help us all get "off the treadmill," to protect us all from continuous work, to help us pull our lives together again. It is a time to enjoy the fruits of creation, a time of rest and restoration. In Exodus 23 God commands, "Six days do your work, but on the seventh day do not work, so that your ox and your donkey may rest and the slave born in your household, and the alien as well, may be refreshed" (v. 12).

That same passage tells us that the land also needs a time of rest. "For six years you are to sow your fields and harvest the crops, but during the seventh year let the land lie unplowed and unused. Then the poor among your people may get food from it, and the wild animals may eat what they leave" (vv. 10-11).

Was this command problematic for God's Old Testament people? Listen to this discussion from Leviticus 25:20-21: "You may ask, 'What will we eat in the seventh year if we do not plant or harvest our crops?' I will send you such a blessing in the sixth year that the land will yield enough for three years." God was instructing the people not to worry, but to practice his law so that the land would be *fruitful.* "If you follow my decrees and are careful to obey my commands, I will send you rain in its season, and the ground will yield its crops and the trees of the field their fruit" (Lev. 26:3-4).

In the New Testament, Christ clearly defines the place of the sabbath in our lives: The sabbath is made for we who are served by it, not the other way around. The sabbath is made for the land, for the people, and for God's other creatures. Thus, the sabbath year is given to protect the land from relentless exploitation, to help the land rejuvenate, to help it pull itself together again.

This sabbath is not merely a legalistic requirement; rather, it is a profound principle. That's why in some farming communities the sabbath principle is practiced by letting the land rest every *second* year, because "that is what the land needs." The sabbath is made for the land, and not the land for the sabbath. The sabbath rule is not therefore restricted to agriculture but applies to all creation. It affects our use of water and air. It has implications for where we discharge our exhaust, smoke, sewage, and other things that we "throw away."

God speaks strongly on this issue through the Word:

> If you will not listen to me and carry out all these commands, and
> if you reject my decrees and abhor my laws and fail to carry out
> all my commands and so violate my covenant. . . . your land will
> be laid waste, and your cities will lie in ruins. Then the land will en-
> joy its sabbath years all the time that it lies desolate . . . the land

will have the rest it did not have during the sabbaths you lived in it.

—Leviticus 26:14-15, 33-35

These are harsh words from the holy Creator who is concerned for the world. But God's promises of blessing are equally powerful for those who heed his words:

If you keep your feet from breaking the sabbath and from doing as you please . . . then you will find your joy in the LORD, and I will cause you to ride on the heights of the land. . . .

—Isaiah 58:13-14

Principle 4
We should enjoy, but must not destroy, creation's fruitfulness.

God's blessing of fruitfulness is for the fish of the sea and the birds of the air as well as for people. In Genesis 1 God declares, "Let the water teem with living creatures, and let birds fly above the earth across the expanse of the sky" (v. 20). And then God blesses these creatures with fruitfulness: "Be fruitful and increase in number and fill the water in the seas, and let the birds increase on the earth" (v. 22).

God's evident hand in creation reflects a commitment to providing for the land and life on earth. Psalm 104 depicts God's care for the world:

He makes springs pour water into the ravines; it flows between the mountains. They give water to all the beasts of the field; the wild donkeys quench their thirst. The birds of the air nest by the waters; they sing among the branches. He waters the mountains from his upper chambers; the earth is satisfied by the fruit of his work.

—vv. 10-13

And Psalm 23 describes how our providing God ". . . makes me lie down in green pastures . . . leads me beside quiet waters . . . restores my soul."

As God's work brings fruit to creation, so should ours. As God provides for the creatures, so should we people who were created to reflect God whose image we bear. Imaging God, we too should provide for the creatures. And, as Noah spared no time, expense, or reputation when God's creatures were threatened with extinction, neither should we. In Noah's time a deluge of water covered the land. In our time a deluge of people sprawls over the land, displacing God's creatures, limiting *their* potential to obey God's command to "be fruitful and increase in number." To those who would allow a human flood to roll across the land at the expense of all other creatures, the prophet Isaiah warns: "Woe to you who add house to house and join field to field till no space is left and you live alone in the land" (Isa. 5:8).

Thus, while we are expected to enjoy creation, and while we are expected to partake of creation's fruit, we may not destroy the fruitfulness upon which creation's fullness depends. We must, with Noah, save the species whose interactions with each other, and with land and water, form the fabric of the biosphere. We must let the profound admonition of Ezekiel 34:18 reverberate and echo in our minds: "Is it not enough for you to feed on the good pasture? Must you also trample the rest of your pasture with your feet? Is it not enough for you to drink clear water? Must you also muddy the rest with your feet?"

Principle 5
We must seek first the kingdom of God.

Our culture today proclaims its insistent message: "Seek ye first a job, and then the kingdom will be added unto you." It is tempting to yield to this message and to follow those whose highest priority is to accumulate immense material gain. But Jesus advises us, in Matthew 6:33, to seek first the kingdom of God and God's rightness. And then, Jesus says, as a consequence of seeking God's kingdom, everything else that we need will be given to us as well.

Personal happiness, joy, and fulfillment are not what we seek first of all in life. Instead we seek the kingdom of God and strive toward making God's creation freshly refined and renewed. When we work toward this end, we discover that happiness and joy are *by-products* of our stewardship; fulfillment comes as a *result* of seeking the kingdom.

Who will inherit this kingdom? Those who seek it as their first and all-consuming priority. Its inheritance is not for those who arrogantly exploit their neighbors, the land, and earth's creatures for all they are worth. Nor is it for those who through their careless and overt actions destroy the earth. The inheritance of these arrogant individuals is death.

But how about those who tend to God's creation in meek humility? Christ confirms their inheritance in Matthew 5:5 when he preaches, "Blessed are the meek, for they will inherit the earth."

Revelation 11:18 sums this up with its solemn and ominous, yet auspicious, message:

> *The nations were angry; and your wrath has come. The time for judging the dead, and for rewarding your servants the prophets and your saints and those who reverence your name, both small and great—and for destroying those who destroy the earth.*

Seeking God's kingdom first is our calling, our vocation. We affirm this calling each time we speak the words of the prayer that Jesus taught us: "Our Father in heaven, hallowed be your name, your kingdom come, your will be done *on earth.* . . ."

Principle 6
We must seek true contentment.

Genesis 1 through 11 and our own experience tell us that, even from the time of Adam and Eve, humanity has not been satisfied with the fruitfulness and grace of the Garden—the productive and beautiful creation that God has provided for us. Since the beginning of time people have chosen to go their own way, grasping more and ever more from the creation for selfish advancement. In our modern age we feel the effects of this relentless urge to press land and life to produce more, ever more, without limit. As we have seen, this drive is seriously degrading the earth's environment today. Our prayer should be that of Psalm 119:36: "Turn my heart toward your statutes and not toward selfish gain."

If searching for contentment through accumulating the goods of creation is harmful, then where do we find true happiness? By doing the work that God would have us do in his world. 1 Timothy 6:6 says, "godliness with contentment is great gain." True contentment means aiming to have the things that will sustain us, but not going beyond that. An Amish saying based on this passage goes like this: "To desire to be rich is to desire to have more than what we need to be content."

Why is it important not to pass the point of contentment? In the words of 1 Timothy 6:11, by not passing this point we can "pursue righteousness, godliness, faith, love, endurance, and gentleness." Hebrews 13:5 puts it this way: "Keep your lives free from the love of money and be content with what you have, because God has said, 'Never will I leave you; never will I forsake you.'"

Being content also helps us preserve creation's integrity. All the things we use, all the things we make, everything we manipulate, everything we accumulate, derives from the creation itself. If we learn to seek godly contentment as our great gain, we will take and shape less of God's earth. We will demand less from the land. We will leave room for the other creatures. We will responsibly exercise dominion over the earth and will preserve it. We will thus allow creation to heal itself and to perpetuate its fruitfulness, to the praise of its Creator.

Principle 7
We must practice what we believe.

Finally, the Scriptures admonish us to *act* on what we know is right. Merely knowing God's requirements for stewardship is not enough. Merely believing in God is not enough, for the Scriptures tell us that even Satan believes in God. Unless we act on our belief and put God's requirements to use, they do absolutely no good.

The inactivity of God's people is well-documented and questioned in the pages of Scripture:

My people come to you, as they usually do, and sit before you to listen to your words, but they do not put them into practice. With their mouths they express devotion, but their hearts are greedy for unjust gain. Indeed, to them you are nothing more than one who sings love songs with a beautiful voice and plays an instrument well, for they hear your words but do not put them into practice.
—Ezekiel 33:31-32

Why do you call me "Lord, Lord," and do not do what I say?
—Luke 6:46

Christian environmental stewardship does not end with the last chapter of a book we are reading on the subject. It does not end when we pick up a study book on a different topic. Instead, studying the Bible to learn God's requirements for stewardship of creation marks a beginning point. It brings us directly to the life-and-death question, "Now what must we *do?*"

The prophet Isaiah, in chapter 58, tells us that we must do more than go through the motions. Our devotion to God and to the Word requires us to care for others—to share our food with the hungry, to loosen the chains of injustice, to let the oppressed go free. The challenge of environmental stewardship is to move forth and put what we know and believe into practice.

Suggestions for Group Session

Getting Started

This chapter describes the Word of God as a handbook on how to live rightly on earth. The Bible has much to teach us about right living in relationship to God, to other people, and to all of creation. This chapter opens our minds to the Bible's teachings on caring for the earth with which we are entrusted. It reminds us that the earth and all that it contains belongs to God, and that we have a responsibility to work in the world as God has commanded.

Begin today's session by having each group member read one line from "Our World Belongs to God," quoted below:

As God's creatures we are made in his image
to represent him on earth,
and to live in loving communion with him.
By sovereign appointment we are
earthkeepers and caretakers:
loving our neighbor,
tending the creation,

and meeting our needs.
God uses our skills
in the unfolding and well-being of his world.

You may want to read the following prayer in unison:

Thank you, God, for the beauty of creation. Thank you for the tes-timony it gives of your everlasting power and divinity. Thank you for not leaving us without guidance. We praise you for showing your love and care for creation. We pray that we, as reflections of your image on earth, also may love and care for creation. Help us to take very seriously Scripture's teachings about earthkeeping. In Jesus' name, Amen.

Group Discussion and Activity

From Chapter Three

1. You may want to take a few minutes to review the seven biblical princi-ples listed in this chapter. Do you have questions about any of the prin-ciples or about their biblical basis? Which of the seven principles seemed to speak most convincingly or most urgently to you?

From Your Experience

1. On a scale of 1 (poor) to 10 (excellent), how would you rate your per-sonal stewardship of God's creation? Share your rating and the reasons for it with others in the group, and discuss ways that you could help each other as you strive to do God's will in caring for creation.

2. What are some ways that we can provide for creation's "sabbath rest?"

From the Bible

1. Suppose you were asked to select three verses from the Bible about caring for creation that were to be reproduced on wall plaques. Which ones from this chapter would you choose? Can you think of other verses from Scripture that you feel are particularly applicable to this study of creation?

2. Read Ezekiel 34:18. How relevant is this passage to the discussion about the abuse of water and land? Does this passage tell us anything about how we should treat the rest of creation? Why or why not?

3. What does Isaiah 5:8 say to us about the way we use land today?

Closing Prayer

Group members can offer brief prayers, thanking God for the Bible, for its depth of meaning, and for what it brings to our lives as we work to live in obedience and love to our Lord. Pray specifically that we might be encouraged to act on what we've learned about earthkeeping, fruitfulness, and sabbath rest for creation.

Note: The next session requires a slow, reflective reading. You'll want to set aside some extra time to thoughtfully consider what it says, because it will provide a theological foundation for understanding what we should be doing as individuals and as the church when it comes to caring for creation.

FOUR

CREATION'S CARE AND KEEPING: A THEOLOGICAL PERSPECTIVE

Introduction

One of the things I remember from my childhood was a comment my parents often made about a sermon that "turned it about." On the way home, following a sermon that deeply probed the Scriptures, a sermon that really "turned it about," my mom and dad would say, "That was a *deep* sermon."

The idea of "turning it about" is an old one. This kind of deep probing and examining is a rabbinical approach to Scripture. A rabbi might ask a student of Scripture to "turn it about, turn it about, for everything you need to know is in it."

In this chapter we will continue searching the Scriptures' teachings on creation and our responsibility, but more deeply. We will "turn it about, turn it about, knowing that everything we need to know is in it!" As we study more deeply, we will have to stop from time to time in our reading to "turn the Scriptures about." For that purpose, this chapter has a new twist. I will write for a time and then take a break to talk with you. These breaks will be typeset in italics. Whenever you read these parts, you can think of these "chatty" comments as my whispering in your ear, much as I might do if we together were listening to a speaker at the podium.

The end of verse 3 in Psalm 75 uses the word *Selah*. This word is used many times in the psalms. *Selah* means you should stop at this point to let things "sink in." You can think of our breaks, my whisperings in your ear, as *Selahs,* but ours require longer pauses and sometimes even a sec-

49

ond reading of the passage in question. We might also use our pauses to check out a point in the previous chapter.

Let's begin at the beginning—at *Bereshith,* as the Bible says in Hebrew—with creation, and even before that!

Creation

The Bible tells us that God created the heavens and the earth (Gen. 1:1). The Heidelberg Catechism, Lord's Day 9, Question 26 also explains that "out of nothing [God] created heaven and earth and everything in them." In Hebrew editions of the Bible, the name given to the book of Genesis is *Bereshith,* which means, "In the beginning." That was when God's Spirit hovered over the waters (Gen. 1:2), and when God created and *crafted* all things through the Word, God's Son (John 1:1-3, 14). God was pleased to have the fullness of divine power dwell in Jesus. Through him all things are sustained (Heb. 1:3) and have their integrity (Col. 1:17; see also Heidelberg Catechism, Lord's Day 10, Questions 27 and 28). During the work of creation, God gave all living creatures an endowment of blessed fruitfulness (Gen. 1:11-12, 20-25, 28) that continues, through Christ, today. When our Creator marked out the foundations of the earth, wisdom was God's craftsman. Wisdom rejoiced in God's whole world; wisdom delighted in humankind (Prov. 8:22-30).

Pause a moment here and let that sink in! Look at the words "crafted" and "craftsman." Think of what it is like before creation. Think about who is present before the beginning. Think about who it is that rejoices in the whole world and its human creatures.

The whole of creation, including each of God's creatures and every human being, belongs to God (Lev. 25:23; Deut. 10:14; 1 Sam. 2:8b; Ps. 24:1; Rom. 14:7-9; 1 Cor. 6:19-20, 10:26). This knowledge provides immeasurable comfort—our *only* comfort in life and in death (Heidelberg Catechism, Lord's Day 1, Question 1).

We are not to fret or worry about the abuse of creation, for our Sovereign Lord reigns! God is good. So are creation and all of God's creatures—God says so repeatedly and directly in Genesis 1. Our Creator's goodness is everywhere apparent: the bright rays of God's goodness shine forth as the sun warms the earth and as the rain and snow water the mountains. God supplies grass for cattle, provides plants for people to cultivate, gives prey to lions, and renews the face of the earth. The fruit of God's work satisfies the earth (see Ps. 104). God's goodness is not "goodiness" of course; creation reflects God's glory in fearsome storms (Ps. 29) and in non-lovable behemoths who boldly dwell in swampy habitats (Job 40:15-24).

Pause for another rest here. Using your Bible, check out any two of the Bible passages cited. Then reread what you have just read. (You are now getting into the discipline of "turning it about.")

Stewardship of Creation

Human beings are called to serve *('abad)* and keep *(shamar)* the garden in the goodness and fruitfulness of God's creation (Gen. 2:15). People are called by God to be earthkeepers.

When God created humans, "God said, 'Let us make man in our image, in our likeness'" (Gen. 1:26). Prior to their disobedience, God asked these human creatures to image their Creator's sustaining rule over earth and to reflect God's righteous integrity and steadfast love (Gen. 1:26-28). Such reflective living—living rightly to bless and keep creation—was done in the light of the Lord of integrity who blesses and keeps his people (cf. Num. 6:24-26).

After their disobedience, such keeping was no longer natural for humans. Since the fall, humans have needed to be told and reminded of what such stewardship means. As the first humans in the Garden came to know their sin, so must we become "conscious of sin" through the Law (Rom. 3:20; 7:7-25).

Now, turn it about!

Alienation from God and Creation

In choosing to know good and evil, in falling away, human beings became aliens both to the Garden and to their Creator.

Today we humans follow our alienated forebears. We are disciples of the first Adam. The consequences of this loyalty for creation, as we saw in Chapter Two, are overwhelming. Pursuing self-interest and greed, people now go for all they can get and create things that are "bigger than life." We abuse creation, and creation groans in ways now everywhere evident.

Disciples of the first Adam (and Eve) need explicit commands and teachings on stewardship and on selfless exercise of dominion. Human beings, now alienated from creation, need specific laws, warnings, and correctives in order to fulfill their tasks as keepers of creation. Among these are the biblical teachings on restoration, fruitfulness, contentment, kingdom priority, and obedience to God.

Restoration

God's *Torah* states, "When you enter the land I am going to give you, the land itself must observe a sabbath to the LORD" (Lev. 25:2b; cf. Ex. 23:11). This means that earth's land and creatures are not to be pressed relentlessly or pushed for all they are worth for human financial or material gain. Instead, honoring the will of their Creator, humans must give land and creatures their time for rest, rejuvenation, and re-creation (see Lev. 25-26 and Ex. 23:10-12).

This should sound familiar; it connects with Principle 3 in the last chapter.

Fruitfulness

"Is it not enough for you to feed on the good pasture? Must you also trample the rest of your pasture with your feet? Is it not enough for you to drink clear water? Must you also muddy the rest with your feet?" (Ezek. 34:18).

Perhaps this verse is still reverberating in your mind from the previous chapter.

While God blesses people with fruitfulness and expects people to enjoy the fruit of creation, we do not have license to destroy the earth (cf. Rev. 11:18) or to destroy its fruitfulness (Deut. 20:19-20; 22:6-7). The Creator proclaims, "Let the water teem with living creatures, and let birds fly above the earth and across the expanse of the sky" (Gen. 1:20). Our blessing must not be the occasion to deny the rest of creation its blessing, for "God blessed them and said, 'Be fruitful and increase in number and fill the water in the seas, and let the birds increase on the earth'" (Gen. 1:22). Isaiah adds his warning when he says, "Woe to you who add house to house and join field to field till no space is left and you live alone in the land" (Isa. 5:8).

Concern for earth's creatures is reflected in God's command to Noah. Genesis 6-9 reviews God's command that Noah prevent the extinction of earth's creatures, both economic and uneconomic, no matter what the cost.

Reflect on all of this; turn it about! Compare Psalm 59 and 75.

Contentment

The Scriptures advise, ". . . Be content with what you have, because God has said, 'Never will I leave you; never will I forsake you'" (Heb. 13:5). We know that the fruitfulness and the gifts of creation did not satisfy Adam or his disciples (Gen. 3-11), but we as God's people should seek ". . . godliness with contentment" as a "great gain" (1 Tim. 6:6). A consequence of human contentment is that creation is less pressed, since all the material things we use and have in our possession come from God through creation.

Rather than turning our hearts toward getting things for ourselves, we are to direct our hearts toward God's statutes (Ps. 119:36). Paul, who "learned the secret of being content in any and every situation" (Phil. 4:12b), provides a detailed description of contentment (1 Tim 6:6-21; cf. Jesus' words in Matt. 6:25-34).

Think again about Principle 6 in the last chapter.

Kingdom Priority

While the world says, "seek first jobs and money, and the kingdom shall be added unto you," Christ turns it around when he tells us ". . . seek first his kingdom and his righteousness, and all these things will be given to you as well" (Matt. 6:33). Fulfillment is a *consequence* of seeking the kingdom. So we must look to the interests of the kingdom first, not to ourselves.

We may be tempted to follow in the steps of those who seek first to accumulate land and other wealth—usually to creation's detriment. In such times, we must seek God's kingdom and hope in the Lord. The Scriptures say, "Trust in the LORD and do good; dwell in the land and enjoy safe pasture. . . . Those who hope in the Lord will inherit the land" (Ps. 37:3, Matt. 5:5; also see Heidelberg Catechism, Lord's Day 48, Question 123).

Recall Principle 5 from the last chapter.

Obedience to God

"Blessed are they whose ways are blameless, who walk according to the law of the LORD. Blessed are they who keep his statutes and seek him with all their heart" (Ps. 119:1-2). The Scriptures tell us that people who are obedient to God, those who walk according to God's law, are blessed. This is true for everyone—for "kings of earth and all the people." Thus the *Torah* tells us that when the king "takes the throne of his kingdom, he is to write . . . a copy of this law. . . . It is to be with him, and he is to read it all the days of his life so that he may learn to revere the LORD his God . . ." (Deut. 17:18-19).

Those who hold the office of king and rule over some part of creation (and that includes all of us) must be so steeped in God's Law that every choice and action is thoroughly consistent with the Law and with the ordinances by which creation is ordered and sustained. The time is coming, declares the Lord, that "I will put my law in their minds and write it on their hearts" (Jer. 31:33; Heb. 8:10, 10:16).

Our model for obedience and obedient service is Jesus Christ, "Who, being in very nature God, did not consider equality with God something to be grasped, but made himself nothing, taking the very nature of a servant. . . . He humbled himself and became obedient to death—even death on a cross!" (Phil. 2:6-8).

Creation's Evangelical Testimony

Despite the abuse humans have inflicted on it, creation clearly witnesses to its Creator. God "has not left himself without testimony: He has shown kindness by giving you rain from heaven and crops in their seasons; he provides you with plenty of food and fills your hearts with joy" (Acts 14:17). While Jesus expects his disciples to "Go into all the world and preach the good news to all creation" (Mark 16:15), creation itself proclaims God's everlasting power and divinity, leaving people "without excuse" (Rom. 1:20). This is summarized in the Belgic Confession, Article 2:

We know [God] by two means:
First, by the creation, preservation, and government
of the universe,
since that universe is before our eyes
like a beautiful book

in which all creatures,
great and small,
are as letters
to make us ponder
the invisible things of God:
   his eternal power
   and his divinity. . . ."

         —From a translation based upon the French text of
         1619 and published in Ecumenical Creeds
         and Reformed Confessions *(Grand Rapids,*
         Michigan: CRC Publications, 1988).

The loud-proclaiming silent heavens give evangelical witness to God's glory (Psalm 19:1-4) and creation pours forth praise to its Creator (Psalm 95-100). God has given us this testimony "so that [we] would seek him and perhaps reach out for him and find him, though he is not far from each one of us" (Acts 17:27).

Think deeply about what you have just read!

Creation is God's greatest and most persistent evangelist. Yet as we see all around us, its evangelical testimony is being diminished in our day. In many of our cities, it no longer makes sense to stand under the night sky and read Psalm 19. Neither does the singing of the second line of the doxology, "Praise God, all creatures here below," ring forth with the same meaning it once had. Creation is degraded at the hands and instruments of fallen people. Human beings are alienated from creation by human actions and constructs that separate them from other creatures.

And this brings to modern disciples of Jesus an auspicious priestly task: to remove the blinders that separate us from creation's testimony to God's everlasting power and divinity, and to restore this testimony where it has been impoverished. This also brings God to the most marvelous expression of love: to give of himself for the world.

God's Love and Reconciliation

God loves the world! This is the clear message of that central proclamation of the New Testament, John 3:16. God's love for the world is so great that he gave his only Son to suffer and die to atone for the world's sin. Christ reconciles *all* things. God affirmed this material world by sending the Son into it. The One who came is the One whose personal creative work brought this world into being and who sustains the world, even today.

All of creation looks with eager expectation for the coming of God's children (cf. Rom. 8:18-21). It looks forward to a renewed material creation that has been refined by the Refiner's fire (Zech. 13:9, Mal. 3:3) that removes as dross the sinful degradation inflicted by Adam and his disciples.

Turn it about! And check at least one Bible reference.

54

Gratitude and Service

Out of gratitude for God's love, God's sustaining care, and God's reconciliation of the world, we join with all creation to serve and praise our maker. We confess that we, as disciples of the first Adam, have abused creation, that we are guilty beyond our own ability to compensate, and that our sin and misery are very great.

But as children of God we also profess that we have abandoned the leadership of the first Adam. We have become disciples of the last Adam—Jesus Christ (for a full discussion of Jesus Christ as second Adam, see the chapter by Ronald Manahan in *Environment and Christian*). We profess that God's sustaining love and reconciliation of the world has also enveloped us, setting us free from sin and misery. And this freedom opens our lives so that we become living testimonies of gratitude to God. By so doing we honor God as Creator and image God's goodness, God's sustaining care for all creation, and God's reconciliation of all things.

Our gratitude to God means that we will not fail to act on what we know is right. See Principle 7 in the last chapter.

As living testimonies of gratitude to God, we work with Christ to undo the works of the first Adam and to accomplish what the first Adam was supposed to do (cf. Matt. 5:16 and Heidelberg Catechism, Lord's Day 32, Question 86). As living testimonies of gratitude, our churches proclaim God's holy and divine Word. They become "Creation Awareness Centers" that open human eyes to the universe as that most elegant book in which all creatures, great and small, make us ponder and see clearly the invisible things of God, even God's eternal power and divinity. Thus, while we take enormous comfort in the fact that we and all of creation belong to God, we cannot be indifferent to creation's abuse, to its impoverished ability to bring God praise, and to our own alienation from creation's testimony.

What then must we do?

- We must be prophets to the world, recognizing and describing our abusive behavior and its consequences for creation.

- We must be priests to the world, unveiling and restoring creation's evangelical witness to God's eternal power and divinity where it has been obscured by abuse and alienation.

- We must be kings over the world, as disciples of the last Adam, Jesus Christ, to set things right in creation.

In short, we must so behave on earth that heaven will not be a shock to us. We must make our lives living reflections of our Lord's prayer, "Thy kingdom come, thy will be done, on earth. . . ."

Suggestions for Group Session

Getting Started

This is not an easy session, but we end the session knowing that God the Creator is still in control. This truly is God's world, no matter what we may have done or may do to it. As a group, begin this session by reading in unison the following words from "Our World Belongs to God":

In all our strivings
to excuse
or save ourselves,
we stand condemned
before the God of truth.
But our world
broken and scarred,
still belongs to God.
He holds it together
and gives us hope.

In your opening prayer, thank God for the great depth of the Scriptures and for the richness that the study of Scripture brings to our understanding of God's will for our lives and for creation. Give thanks for God's gift of the second Adam, and pray that increasingly we might discover what it means to follow the One who made, upholds, and reconciles all things.

Group Discussion and Activity

In your groups today, relate Scripture to Scripture. Puzzle over the meaning of the Bible's identification of Christ as the last Adam. Wonder together about the significance of creation as evangelist. And together become better rooted in the ecological teachings of the Bible.

From Chapter Four

1. Chapter Four called for us to spend some time reflecting on the care and keeping of creation from a theological perspective. The intent was to give us a solid footing in the ecological teachings of the Bible. Please share with the group your general reactions to this process, as well as any insights you gained from your reading and study.

2. How is creation like an "evangelist"? Have you found this to be true in your own experience? Please comment.

3. With other group members, make a list of actions you might take regarding creation if you were a disciple of the first Adam. Then make a contrasting list of actions you might take regarding creation if you were a disciple of the last Adam.

4. Discuss the difference between the following motivations for the care and keeping of creation: gratitude, obedience, love, guilt. What difference does our motivation behind caring for the earth make?

From Your Experience

1. A student I know came back from observing the Kirtland's warbler, an endangered species of bird that nests only in a small area of jack pines near Mio, Michigan. She was asked what she thought about the conservationists' efforts to maintain this species. The student replied, "That's an awful lot of money to spend on a silly little bird." In reply the questioner said, "Yes, the price of gopher wood is very high these days!" What is the connection? Discuss the issues this raises, and substantiate your arguments biblically.

From the Bible

1. According to Acts 17:27, why has God revealed himself to the world in creation? What role, if any, does creation play in our going to all the world to preach the gospel to every creature?

2. The manager of a major Northwest logging company and an environmental scientist discussed the topic "Jobs vs. the Spotted Owl." The manager described how in earlier times two people were needed to operate a handsaw. Later only one person was needed to run a chain saw. Now, he said, many of the trees in the forest are cut by a machine that grabs the trunk, cuts it, strips off the branches, and stacks it on a truck. "We have come to the point now where one person can cut on average one acre of forest each day!"

"Labor-saving technology," replied the environmental scientist.

"Yes," the manager replied.

"What would you rather deal with," asked the scientist, "machines or people?"

"Machines," the manager replied. "People get sick, go on strike, and cannot be used as collateral."

"So, you are cutting more and more, faster and faster, with fewer people?" asked the scientist.

"Yes," was the manager's reply.

"And where does the spotted owl fit into all of this?" asked the scientist.

Replied the manager, "I think I have told you everything you need to know."

What is going on here? What does the manager mean, and what is he really telling the scientist? What is the scientist up to? And where *does* the spotted owl fit into all of this? Does biblical and theological thinking help in resolving the questions this issue raises? If so, how? If not, why not? Should we cut more old-growth forests to protect and create more jobs?

3. Leviticus 25 talks about giving the land a sabbath rest every seventh year. A farmer friend of mine in Neerlandia, Alberta, lets the land rest every second year. By so doing he maintains that he is giving the land its sabbath rest. He has found that this is what the land needs. What do you think of his application of Scripture here?

4. Think for a few minutes about what other applications the sabbath rest has for our lives. Must it be restricted only to farming? Why or why not? If not, then to what does it apply? How do the Bible's other teachings on the Sabbath help put this passage into perspective?

Closing Prayer

To close your session today, show your gratitude to God for the richness of God's revelation in creation and in the Bible. Thank God also for minds with which we can assimilate biblical truth and put it into practice. Pray that our Lord will prepare us to put our knowledge of God's will for creation into practice.

FIVE

RAISING ENVIRONMENTAL AWARENESS IN THE CHURCH

What can we as a church do to respond to environmental concerns? Once we've looked at environmental issues from a Christian perspective, we can no longer sit passively on the sidelines and watch as God's creation is abused. The church needs not only to be aware of the problems but also to seek solutions. Honoring God as Creator, and imaging God's care for creation, the church and its members have a very important contribution to make to our world today in raising awareness on environmental issues.

We need to answer some of the following questions:

- How do we take what we have learned and help our church catch the vision for caring for creation?

- With the vision in place, how can we put what we know into practice?

- How can we keep this vision constantly before the church?

This chapter will help to address these questions, but not by providing a simple prescription. Rather, this chapter will provide a technique for mining the best ideas out of the minds of all members of the congregation— children and adults, clergy and laity, male and female, rich and poor, teacher and student, urbanite and farmer. The church can become increasingly a part of the solution.

As churches become aware of the environmental crisis, a growing number of them are becoming "Creation Awareness Centers." They are seeking to demonstrate the responsibility and privilege they have to be good stewards of creation. Each church can develop plans that attempt to meet the opportunities and necessities that the local situation presents, and to assess regional and global needs as well. Some will want to make use of other churches' environmental awareness programs as models.

In this chapter I present a procedure for implementing creation awareness that gets beyond the up-front "negatives": "Is this something we should be doing?" "Do we have the necessary time?" "Do we have the necessary funds?" This procedure also provides a vehicle for bringing specific, organized ideas from the members to the decision makers in the church. The church council or Creation Awareness Committee can thus benefit from the undiluted strengths, talents, and abilities of the congregation.

The procedure works best with a group of eight to fifty people who already share a concern for and understanding of environmental issues and creation abuse. A one-hour session usually is sufficient to identify and screen ideas. Following the session, results should be summarized and put together in a document for distribution to members of the congregation, committees, and pastors for further development and implementation.

Since this process takes advantage of the particular situation and available talents of a congregation, each resulting Creation Awareness Center will have its own personality and character.

Procedure

A. General Setting and Room Arrangement

Set up the room with all chairs in a single circle. Remove extra chairs from the circle, but keep them close at hand for any latecomers. Bring a supply of note cards or similar-sized recycled or minimum-impact sheets. Keep pencils or pens available for any members who come without them.

B. "Diversity Generator"

When group members are seated, give each one two blank note cards. They should use only one side of the card when they start to write. Begin with the premise that God must be honored as Creator and Sustainer of this world. Then ask yourselves this question: "What specific ideas can we think of to make our church a Creation Awareness Center?" Have each person write one specific idea on one of the cards.

Following are some questions to consider as you reflect on this assignment:

- What is our situation here? What local environmental problems need to be addressed?

- How can this congregation become a kind of "window on creation," a model of how to care for God's earth?

- What unique talents do we have in our congregation that could contribute to creation awareness?

- What could our special contributions be toward the care and keeping of creation?

- How can we best meet the needs of creation and raise awareness?

When most of the members have finished writing (about three to five minutes), think of another idea and write it on the other card. Exercise your deepest and most creative thinking. Move beyond the obvious.

C. "Idea Skimmer"

After group members have finished recording their ideas, have them pass both cards to their right. Repeat this step so the cards have been passed twice. Each person should then carefully read both of the cards in their hands. After a minute or so, each person should pass the card with the better idea to the person on their right and keep the card with the weaker idea. If both ideas are of equal merit, select either one to pass.

Next, each person should evaluate their two ideas again and prepare to pass the better one to the right. When all participants are ready, pass again. Repeat this procedure three to seven times. This process sifts the best ideas by passing them through a screen of different perspectives. The best ideas will naturally pass the test of enduring different viewpoints.

When you've decided as a group that you're done passing cards, each person should read aloud the better of the two ideas in his or her possession. Continue around the circle until each person has read one idea, and put the cards that were read from together in a pack.

D. More Ideas

Pass out another blank card to each group member. Taking into account the ideas that were read before in the circle, identify additional ideas that could help make the church a Creation Awareness Center. Some categories to think about:

- liturgy, sermons, songs, order of worship
- church building, grounds
- region, state, nation, world
- animals, plants, woods, fields, parks, streets
- global atmospheric problems, soil degradation, deforestation, animal and plant extinction, surface water and groundwater degradation, local and global toxification, and human cultural abuses.

Repeat the passing procedure used previously, again passing to the right from three to seven times, concluding with the reading of the better ideas. Collect each card right after it is read and put it in a second pack.

E. Filling Remaining Gaps

Share any important idea that has not yet been read. Then collect these cards, putting them in a third pack.

F. Cataloging Ideas

Together as a group (or assigning this task to two or three persons), you will want to prepare a document based on the contents of the three card packs. Identify major topics and sort the cards into these categories. Categories might be Creation Awareness Committee, other congregational committees, administration, liturgy and worship, building and grounds, community, and so on. Arrange the categories in a logical order, with those that address the Creation Awareness Center at the top. Type up the ideas by categories, and add a descriptive title to your document.

Distribution of the Results and Follow-Up

The procedure described above is one way of helping a church come to grips with issues of environmental abuse and stewardship and learning how to deal with them. But generating ideas and selecting and cataloging the best ones will not make the church a Creation Awareness Center. The next logical step is *action*.

After obtaining necessary approvals, distribute the document to those who should receive it. You may also want to consider printing the results in the congregational newsletter or in the bulletin as an insert. Follow up by examining each of the categories, bringing the content of each category to the attention of the pastor, stewardship coordinator, and appropriate committees and task forces. Use the document together as you take the steps needed to make your church a Creation Awareness Center.

Ideas Gleaned from Congregations

STOP! The following lists of ideas should not be consulted until after your group has generated its own ideas. These lists are an edited compilation of group results from several congregations who used the procedure described above.

A. Creation Awareness Committee

1. Form a Creation Awareness Committee to instill an understanding of God as Creator and to assist people in becoming better stewards of our Lord's creation.

2. Publish information on Christian environmental stewardship in the church newsletter.

3. Place books and articles on Christian environmental stewardship in the church library, including those with biblical principles, practical suggestions for action, and local natural history and ecology.

4. Provide creation-rich materials for shut-ins and residents of nursing homes, including audiotapes of birds, running waters, and weather; also provide bird-feeders for their windows, and set up a schedule for keeping the feeders filled.

B. Worship and Liturgy

1. Designate one Sunday each season for recognizing our commitment to God's earth.

2. Request a sermon on creation stewardship and earthkeeping.

3. Request that the minister preach on Revelation 11:18, "The time has come . . . for destroying those who destroy the earth."

4. Devote at least a portion of each worship service to creation awareness. (For example, each week have at least one family report on something they are doing to help take care of or to preserve God's creation.)

5. Encourage church leaders and members to extend the principle of compassion to all living things (human beings, animals, flora, fauna, and the biosphere).

6. Hold a well-planned outdoor worship service on environmental stewardship in a park or in an awe-inspiring creation setting, followed by a picnic.

7. Plan a multigenerational half-day or even a two-hour field trip to regain excitement for God's creation. Include such things as star gazing or delighting in the life of a river.

8. Plant a new church whose mission statement would direct that all members practice stewardship and promote and honor the Lord of creation in every respect. (The "Lord of Creation Church" would give Article 2 of the Belgic Confession particular attention.)

C. Church Building and Grounds

1. Use a church sign that emphasizes the importance of caring for creation.

2. Have an energy audit to find out how the church could use energy more efficiently.

3. Use energy-efficient lighting and lighting that turns itself off when people are not present and when window light is adequate.

4. Assign someone the responsibility to make sure all lights, fans, and air conditioning are turned off when the church building is empty.

5. Remodel as necessary to save energy: insulate the building, add solar units, put in a heat-pump water heater, and install dropped ceilings where appropriate.

6. Place and designate recycling bins in the church kitchen for sorting tin cans, glass, and aluminum foil. Recycle paper in the church office and bulletins at back of church. Put up a sign in the kitchen to remind people of the church's recycling program.

7. Provide within the church building various displays and decorations that will serve as continual reminders of God's creation, the marvelous diversity and variety of life, and God's care and keeping of us and all creatures. Place these as banners in the sanctuary or as pictures and wall-hangings in the fellowship hall and classrooms.

8. Make provisions in the church building that will encourage members to appreciate creation: make sure the windows open, and place clear glass panes in appropriate locations.

9. Develop a naturally self-sustaining park (garden) where people of the community can sit in peace and quiet, enjoy creation, and commune with the Creator. Have a sign at the entrance to your miniature "Garden of Eden" that states the purpose of the park. Plant berry bushes and trees that will attract a greater variety of birds and animals.

10. Add an open-air, covered picnic area to the church grounds.

11. Add a rain-filled irrigation tank for watering plantings inside and outside of the church building.

12. Encourage your congregation to use alternate methods to travel to church. Aim for a parking lot that has as many bicycles as cars. Let it be known that arriving at church by bicycle or by walking is all right. (Following this idea would mean that more casual clothing would be accepted and considered appropriate.)

Must be Convicted to do all of this

D. Congregational Education

1. Make use of the books and articles you placed in the church library that focus on creation awareness for different age groups. Make them a part of your curriculum for all age groups.

2. Identify your church's connection to its environment: What materials are the products that we use made of? Where does our food come from? Where does our waste go?

3. Hold a six- or seven-week mini-series to explain the degradations of creation. Most people are unaware of the *actual* problems. Some sessions could be used to develop ideas to right the wrongs.

4. Provide the pastor(s) and teachers with an opportunity to complete a special course of study dealing specifically with responsibility to the creation.

5. Develop service projects that involve families: planting flowers and trees, starting recycling programs for the elderly, adopting a highway stewardship program, or speaking about stewardship to different area churches.

6. Serve as a host for children from a particular city church for one week. Show them the wonders of God's creation in a country setting. (Or vice versa.)

7. Involve church members in activities that support local agricultural efforts in soil stewardship, such as contour cropping, intensive rotational grazing, reduced chemical inputs, and improved animal care.

8. Fund and support members of your church to act as environmental stewards to debate and influence public policy in the interest of maintaining and restoring creation's integrity.

E. Stewardship Education for Congregation and Community

1. Invite people in your community to be part of your "Creation Awareness Center."

2. Offer community education classes on the how, what, and where of recycling in your area. Become an information center for source reduction and recycling in the broadest sense.

3. Provide information on environmentally sound practices, such as efficient thermostat setting, use of electric coffee-makers, and proper disposal of home cleansers, batteries, plastics, petroleum-based products, and organic matter.

4. Establish a forum/education/support group for farmers, gardeners, business people, and homemakers who are wrestling with stewardship issues so that these people don't feel alone in their stewardship efforts.

5. Make an inventory of all plant and animal communities within a half-mile radius of the church. This inventory should be displayed pictorially as an exhibit.

6. Organize annual or semi-annual "Creation Rehabilitation Workdays" where members work on planting trees, cleaning up a stretch of highway, landscaping a vacant lot, or buying some land and protecting it.

7. Arrange for a local supermarket to display produce along the sidewalk and storefront to bring the produce closer to the outdoor world, as was done in earlier days.

8. Reclaim a piece of land—an urban park, city block, or some other area and take care of it, modeling stewardship and involving the area residents. Or adopt a wetland or woodland, keeping it, caring for it, and using it to educate yourselves and others.

9. Take a field trip to the local landfill to show people the waste we generate in our society.

F. Study Groups, Youth, and Christian Education

1. With the others in your congregation, approach Bible study with an openness to receive the message of creation, the Creator, and creation's care and keeping.

2. Hold Vacation Bible School at a local county park, or hold the final celebration at a park with a potluck following. Bring students on walks for the purpose of discovering creation, learning awe and wonder, and developing an understanding of caring for creation.

3. Start an environmental awareness program with church school participants, involving them in a different environmental clean-up or awareness project each month.

4. Make creation awareness part of the church school curriculum. Teach lessons for the children about the need to preserve our world, and provide practical instruction in how to do this.

G. Congregational Life and Response

1. As a congregation you must commit yourselves to live out your faith through caring for that part of God's creation in which you live. For example, commit to caring for a nearby creek or watershed, adopting a highway or endangered species, recycling the garbage you produce, and keeping your cars as environmentally fit as possible.

2. Arrange for informal meetings of church families at the local county park on a regular schedule. Invite individuals who can help people see and interpret their natural surroundings.

3. Initiate a program that involves all family members in conducting whole-family environmental and conservation projects in and around their homes and neighborhoods.

4. Have each individual set a personal goal each month to transform talk into action.

5. Hold a Friday or Saturday evening retreat with nature study and star-watching.

6. Plan a multigenerational tree-planting event involving entire families.

H. Resource Use and Conservation

1. Purchase glass or ceramic dinnerware instead of throwaway paper and plastic products.

2. Use glass communion cups.

3. Arrange to have church committees meet at the same time in order to conserve heating and air conditioning.

4. Adopt a "no chemical use" policy for lawn and plant care.

5. Adopt a "no throwaway" policy for church functions where food and coffee are served.

6. Use cloth tablecloths for church functions.

7. Use recycled paper for church bulletins, publications, and correspondence.

8. Put timers on outside lights.

9. Put motion- and light-detecting wall switches in appropriate places so that lights automatically go out when people are not present or when natural lighting is at high levels.

10. Develop a car pool or mass-transit arrangement for bringing members to church. Also provide bicycle racks. This will reduce the need for a large parking lot, and will allow you to turn part of the parking lot into a park with trees, plants, and flowers.

I. Personal Lives, Lifestyle, and Home

1. Encourage members to turn their homes and workplaces into Creation Awareness Centers.

2. Provide opportunities for each member to commit himself or herself to stating what he or she will do as a steward of creation. Recognize in some concrete way good stewardship in the broader church community.

3. Arrange for a "pedal-power activity" and use it as a basis for discussing how you can help others, yourselves, and creation.

4. Put timers on thermostats to shorten the time your furnace and air conditioning are working.

5. Replace light fixtures and light bulbs with new, energy-efficient ones.

6. Continue to be a witness to others through the example of your own life.

J. Cooperation with Other Churches

1. Invite two other nearby churches to join in you in forming a Creation Awareness Center. Publicize what you are doing to encourage others through television, newspapers, and letters.

2. Work with other churches in the classis or synod to promote creation and environmental awareness in their congregations.

3. Form a team to glean from other churches the best ideas and approaches for making your church into a Creation Awareness Center.

4. Plan a community-wide workshop on God's creation that involves all churches of the community. Follow up with concrete projects on energy conservation, clean-up, materials use, and the like.

5. Conduct a city-wide or classis/synod-wide energy and waste audit of church buildings.

K. Providing Leadership in Society

1. Be leaders in speaking out against creation abuse.

2. Continue efforts with other churches in the community to form a task force to encourage concern about environmental issues.

3. Sponsor environmental improvement such as cleaning up a riverbank, a lakeshore, or a portion of highway.

4. Have members recognize and explain how their occupations negatively impact creation. Brainstorm with other members on how they can work to change the situation.

5. Urge your church's local or national governing body, or indeed, the church universal, to make a statement about creation and the environment that contains practical applications for your daily lives.

L. I'm Not Done Talking Yet!

Here are some more ideas of things you can do to be a good steward of creation:

- build window boxes, roof-top gardens, ground-level gardens
- build fish ponds with fluorescent night lights for insect feeding
- plant edible cultivars and edible flowers (nasturtiums)
- encourage or practice rotational grazing and regenerative gardening
- use native plant restoration, indigenous gardening, and forest garden techniques
- encourage seed and tree distribution
- encourage church lawn conversion
- request liturgical expression, hymnody, and sermons regarding creation
- reclaim creation terminology (creation, creatures)

- reintroduce the Hebrew tradition of singing psalms
- establish walking trails through nature and fields and gardens
- promote environmentally-conscious architecture to allow for window boxes and for the growth of small trees and shrubs
- restore habitats around houses to provide for a large diversity of creatures
- develop lawns with biodiversity that fix their own atmospheric nitrogen and naturally recycle "thatch"
- install windows in the church and home to provide views of the creation
- do your own energy audit
- assist on a farm, buy the beef you eat on the hoof and have it processed
- purchase one hundred acres of tropical rain forest for preservation
- develop a paid summer stewardship mission experience for young people at the wages they might earn as a fast-food clerk
- develop a guided bicycle trip for groups and individuals to see firsthand good and poor stewardship in your community
- make your church a center for distribution of native flowers and trees on Arbor Day
- make your church a distribution center for vegetable seeds and related literature on food and the environment in late spring
- talk with a farmer about planting a crop for direct human consumption; help identify a market for it, and deliver the surplus to a local food pantry
- conduct a gleaning party
- develop a wheelchair nature loop at a local rest home
- conduct a food-source awareness dinner at church
- conduct a hunger awareness dinner at church
- conduct food-label reading sessions
- set up a "vacation trip tithe" in which each family's tenth trip would be to a place where people could use their labor
- encourage a local restaurant to use place mats that show the relationship of menu items to the places where food is grown
- encourage the local newspaper to become involved in environmental issues
- do volunteer weeding for a local gardener
- develop a program to teach people about the lives and adaptations of plants in sidewalk cracks and lawns
- arrange with an artist to do a painting of the heavens to place in your church
- arrange for an "astronomy night" to make Psalm 19 come alive
- take a field trip to a zoo, taking particular note of the hippopotamus; then do a study of Job 40:15ff
- spend forty-five minutes in the fall of the year lying in a forest listening to the leaves fall. Discover for yourself why leaves on the floor of a woods or forest disappear, even when they're not raked.

- put one kernel of corn in a transparent container at the entrance of your church for every additional person there is on earth since last week's service

Suggestions for Group Session

Getting Started

This chapter provides a fresh break from our study by giving us something very important to do. We have come to the point where we can take what we have learned and develop a very practical response by making our church into a Creation Awareness Center.

As we begin this session, group members should spend time in prayer, asking God to help them reflect carefully on what we have learned and to think specifically about ways we can respond as a church. Pray that God will illumine us today to find ways that we can become better aware of creation and find ways to transform our church so that we fully acknowledge our Creator in thought, word, and deed. Pray that we might conduct our lives in such a way that we image God's love for creation.

Group Discussion and Activity

This week we suggest that the group follow the procedure outlined at the beginning of Chapter Five. This will likely take most, if not all, of today's session.

After using the note card procedure, we suggest that the group quickly skim the additional ideas listed in Chapter Five. Perhaps the group will want to add a few of these ideas to the ones they've included in the three stacks of note cards. Please be sure to appoint a subgroup to do the necessary cataloging, writing, and distribution.

* * * * * * * *

Groups that choose not to use the above procedure may instead do the following:

- skim Chapter Five, placing a check mark by those ideas that seem to have some possibility for your congregation
- share all checked ideas with the entire group
- add other ideas that group members generate
- go back through each category and decide which ideas you could actually implement in your congregation
- appoint a subgroup to write up and distribute your findings

Groups may also want to use one or more of the following Bible study questions:

1. Read Psalm 96. How does the psalmist portray the earth—as a living thing or as an inanimate thing?

2. Select one or two phrases from Psalm 96 about creation and explain why you enjoy them.

3. What is the psalm really about, creation or God? Can the world in its present condition really praise God? Explain.

Closing Prayer

Give thanks to God for the testimony of the Scriptures and the testimony of all that God has made. Give thanks too for the minds with which our Creator has endowed us, and for the ideas we have generated using this marvelous gift. Ask God's blessing on those who compile the results of today's session, and pray for the body of Christ that needs to put its faith into action in responsible living in creation.

Be sure that a small group of people are picked to do the final cataloguing of the ideas and to write them up.

Option: Group members may decide not to use the card system. In that case, devise another system for generating and recording ideas. Use newsprint, a blackboard, or overhead transparencies. Compile these ideas into a document that can be distributed later to church members.

SIX

CLEARING AND PREPARING THE WAY[1]

We know that there are lots of things we should do in life, including taking care of creation. But the fact is that we *don't* do many of the things we know we *should* do in life. Often different things stand in our way and make us stumble so that we never get past "square one." Sometimes we encounter holes in the road that not only give us a jolt, but also gobble us up, stopping our journey well before we reach our goal.

To start off this concluding chapter, we will identify the stumbling blocks that may prevent us from taking action. Then we will look at one pitfall to creation's care and keeping that we want to avoid.

Stumbling Blocks to Creation's Care and Keeping

There are quite a number of troublesome stumbling blocks in the way of creation-keeping discipleship for many Christians today. Some of these we have invented ourselves. Others have been devised by our friends. Still others have been devised by our enemies.

We must identify these stumbling blocks so that we can clear them away. Only then can we get down to business and put our beliefs into practice. All of us know these stumbling blocks and most of us have stumbled over some of them. They have kept us from experiencing fully the honor of stewardship under our Creator, Sustainer, and Reconciler.

[1]Most of the material in this session was first published in the *Evangelical Review of Theology*, April, 1993, under the title, "God's love for the world and Creation's environmental challenge to evangelical Christianity."

Some of the major stumbling blocks are outlined below. Each is followed by a comment that might help us remove it from our path.

"This world is not my home, I'm just passing through." (Translation: "Since we are headed for heaven anyway, why take care of creation?")

It is true that those who truly believe on Jesus Christ receive the gift of everlasting life. But this everlasting life began at birth and includes the here-and-now. In this here-and-now we take care of our bodies, our teeth, and our hair. We also take care of our possessions—our clothes, automobiles, and homes. Similarly, we take care of our buildings—even though the largest of these, the skyscrapers, are constructed with a demolition plan on file (to allow their safe destruction a hundred or so years later).

The world that we live in is much more enduring than either our selves, our possessions, or our construction projects. So shouldn't the care of creation also be part of our here-and-now concern? Isn't this the teaching of Revelation 11:18?

"Caring for creation gets us too close to the New Age movement." (Translation: "Isn't concern for the environment and working for a better world what the New Age movement is all about? I don't want people to think I'm a 'New Ager.'")

The Bible, of course, has a lot to say about the created world. It begins by describing in its first few chapters how the world came to be. Those chapters also describe human beings as the earth's caretakers. As Christians we confess that our entire world belongs to God. It is not the private property of any group. We care for creation because God has created it and God has delegated this responsibility to us (Gen. 1:27-30).

"Respecting creation gets us too close to pantheism." (Translation: "If you care for plants and animals, and especially if you value protecting endangered species, you are close to worshiping them as gods.")

Surprisingly, pantheism (creature worship) is a growing problem—even in our scientific age. In our study of creation, we must direct our awe and wonder at God and not at creation. As Paul (Rom. 1:25) and Luke (Acts 14:14-18) teach us, making this distinction is crucial to truly honoring God.

"We need to avoid anything that looks like political correctness." (Translation: "Being 'politically correct' these days means being pro-abortion and pro-environment, and I'll have nothing to do with that.")

The Ku Klux Klan, a racist organization in the United States, uses the symbol of the cross in its terrorizing activities. Does this mean that Christians no longer should use the symbol of the cross on their churches? Some New Age devotees use the symbol of the rainbow in their literature. Does this mean that Christians, who know the rainbow to be the sign of God's covenant with "all living creatures of every kind on earth" (Gen.

9:1-17), should stop using this symbol in their educational materials? People who identify themselves as "politically correct" may advocate saving uneconomic species from extinction. Does this mean that there can be no new Noahs who, in response to God's call to save species from extinction, will act to preserve God's living creatures? We approach the subject of caring for creation as God's stewards, not as members of a politically correct group.

"There are too many worldly people out there doing environmental things." *(Translation: "If people who don't share my beliefs in God and Jesus Christ are working to save the earth, I know it can't be right for me.")*

In Isaiah 45, unbelieving Cyrus is anointed to do God's work. Often if God's people are unwilling or unable to do God's work, God sees to it that the work gets done nonetheless. We must not use the fact that there are some worldly people out there caring for creation to excuse ourselves from our God-given task as stewards of God's creation.

"Caring for creation will lead to world government." *(Translation: "If we try to tackle global environmental problems, we'll have to cooperate with other nations. Won't that help set the stage for world government?")*

There is no doubt that cooperation (with unbelievers and with other nations) will be necessary in order to address many of our environmental problems. Migrating birds, for example, do not recognize international boundaries. Their care may involve the cooperation of many nations along their migratory path.

Such cooperation does not have to lead to world government. For example, the work of the International Crane Foundation to care for wetland habitats and birds has been accomplished through cooperation between the individual nations of Russia and China and between North Korea and South Korea. The end result has not been a world government.

"Before you know it, we will have to support abortion." *(Translation: "Because of the relationship between environmental abuse and growing human population, we will soon find ourselves having to accept abortion as a solution to environmental problems.")*

Our obligation and privilege to care for God's creation does not give us license to use whatever means we have at our disposal to address environmental problems. The fact that many people justify abortion as a population growth control method does not mean that Christians need to see this as a logical solution to environmental abuse.

"I don't want to be an extremist or alarmist." *(Translation: "I want to be considered normal and not some kind of prophet of gloom and doom.")*

Gloom and doom are not necessary components of the message that needs to be brought to creation keepers. Frightening ourselves into action is far less preferable to caring for creation out of gratitude to and love for the

Creator. As for being called an alarmist, is it wrong to sound the fire alarm when a building is burning? Because of the abuses against creation and their drastic consequences, it may be necessary to sound the alarm "before the whole building burns."

"The term dominion means what it says—oppressive domination." (Translation: "I think the Bible says that we have the right to destroy things that get in our way. We can do what we need to do with creation.")

Many people, particularly critics of Christianity, have pointed to Genesis 1:28 as the root cause of our environmental problems. But dominion as outright oppression is not advocated or condoned by the Scriptures.

First, God gave the blessing and mandate of Genesis 1:28 to people *before the fall.* Second, this passage must be understood not in isolation, but in the context of the rest of the Bible. By doing so, one will arrive at the conclusion that the term *dominion* means responsible stewardship, to which the biblical principles presented in this book attest. The Christian model for dominion is the example of Jesus Christ, who was given all dominion. "Being in very nature God . . . [he] made himself nothing, taking the very nature of a servant. . . . he humbled himself and became obedient to death—even death on a cross!" (Phil. 2:6-8).

"People are more important than the environment." (Translation: "I'm for people, and that means that people are more important than saving species of plants and animals. If anything is endangered it is people, not furbished louseworts or snail darters.")

This rationalization is often given for not saving living species that are threatened with extinction. Again we must turn our attention back to what God says in the Bible. We have, of course, an actual instance of God directing that people save animals in the account of the flood (Gen. 6-9). We need to ask the following questions about that story: Who perishes? Who is saved? Are species less important than individual people? Is the environment around people less important than the people this environment supports?

A Pitfall to Creation's Care and Keeping

Across Christendom there is a widely held belief that we come to know God through two major means: special revelation and general revelation. In simplistic terms, special revelation refers to the holy Scripture, comprised of the Old and New Testaments; general revelation refers to God's self-revelation in creation. Through general revelation we discover that God is the author of creation. We could call the created world and the written Word the "two books" of God's revelation.

Most Christians affirm this "two-book" approach to divine revelation. But there have always been some "one-book" Christians who have seen the Bible, or special revelation, as the only means by which God is revealed to us. Such people usually do not remain "one-book" Christians for long because the Bible itself so strongly affirms general revelation.

Conversely, some individuals have become so impressed with how the created world works that they have come to believe that the natural world is the only revelation that has ultimate meaning for our modern day. They too have become "one-book" people. Some people who believe this way describe themselves as "post-Christian." They acknowledge their roots and their "journey" through Christianity, but see themselves as having passed through such thinking. Some of these "one-book" believers see the Bible as a major stumbling block to living rightly on the earth today. They insist that the Bible should be put on the shelf for twenty years while Christians focus on the environment, or that the Bible should be dismissed altogether as totally irrelevant to our world today.

Many of those who confess such "earth-centered spirituality" believe that the church should be enlightened and transformed to their way of thinking as well. The authors of the book *The Reign of Reality* attempt to replace the word "God" with the word "Reality." The "Kingdom of God" is transformed into the "Reign of Reality." This book attempts to deny the authority of the Bible and the presence of a personal God.

"One-book" believers who advocate creation-centered spirituality, true to their earth-centered approach, often describe God as something that emerges from the world as a developing consciousness. For them, God is an emergent property of the evolutionary unfolding of the universe. Christ has been transformed into the "Christ Spirit" that is somehow the expression of the earth's spiritual nature.

The pitfall here is not so much that there is a developing belief around earth-centered spirituality. The pitfall is this: such thinking can easily infiltrate the church. Adherents to this philosophy see it as necessary for the church. They feel driven to wean Christianity away from its trust in the Bible and the personal God of Abraham, Isaac, and Jacob. They feel that believers must be weaned from trusting in Jesus Christ as Lord. Earth itself, they say, will bring a person to maturity through the new light. Thus, the Bible is deemphasized and the Bible is deliteralized.

Those who advocate this kind of spirituality, such as Matthew Fox and Thomas Berry, are doing the best they can to explain the world without a personal God and Savior and without the need for the leading of the Holy Spirit. They have passed through Christianity to evolve into something they consider better, something they believe is in better accord with the ways things truly are.

I know some of the people who hold to this perspective, who attempt to deprecate the Bible, depersonalize God, and transform Jesus Christ into an all-pervasive earth-spirit. I suggest the following remarkably easy means to avoiding this pitfall in our lives and in our churches:

- Continue to pray to God the Father in the name of Jesus Christ.
- Continue to read and believe God's written Word.
- Continue to be willing to be led by the Holy Spirit in your daily walk.

Those who are fully committed to earth spirituality cannot do these things; these activities are contradictory to their beliefs about God, Jesus, and the Bible. They deny the power of the Scriptures to inform us; they deny that we have access through prayer to God who, through our Mediator, can hear and respond to our concerns and petitions; and they deny that the Holy Spirit has power in this world to guide us.

Solutions to Stumbling Blocks and Pitfalls

What must we do about creation?

The simple yet profound response to this question appears to be this: "Love God as Redeemer *and* Creator, acknowledge God's love for the world, and act upon this by following Jesus—the One who creates, upholds, and reconciles all things." We can present this action in the three simple terms that follow:

1. Awareness (seeing, identifying, naming, locating)
2. Appreciation (tolerating, respecting, valuing, esteeming, cherishing)
3. Stewardship (using, restoring, serving, keeping, entrusting)

Our ultimate purpose is to honor God as Creator in such a way that Christian environmental stewardship is part and parcel of everything we do. Our goal is to make tending the garden of creation, in all of its aspects, an unquestioned and all-pervasive aspect of our service to each other, to our community, and to God's world.

Let's deal with each of these three steps as they appear above.

Awareness

Awareness stands at the very beginning as the first of three components of creation stewardship. In a time when so much calls for our attention, the natural aspects of creation may not even seem real to us. We might find that creation seems real only on some of our travels, and even then it may be seriously obscured. We must consciously make ourselves aware of what is happening in God's creation.

Awareness involves seeing, naming, identifying, and locating different parts of creation. It involves taking off our self-imposed or societally-imposed blinders so that we not only see God's creation, but that we want to learn and know the names of the things we see. It involves taking time and having the will to identify a tree or a mountain, a bird or a river. It involves entering the natural world intentionally in order to locate and find God's creatures that we sing about each week in the doxology: "Praise God, all creatures here below."

Appreciation

Awareness is not an end in itself. From awareness comes appreciation. This word *appreciation* covers a whole range of meanings. It may mean nothing more than *toleration*. We may tolerate, for example, worms and hyenas. But appreciation may mean going beyond a mere toleration to *respect*. We certainly respect a large bear, but we also can develop respect for a lowly worm as we learn about its critical importance to the rest of creation. We can also move from toleration to respect to *valuing*. When God was finished creating the world, God said that it was good. The earth and everything in it has value because God made it so. But appreciation can go even beyond valuing to *esteeming* and *cherishing* those things that God holds dear.

Stewardship

Appreciation, though, is not an end in itself either. Appreciation needs to lead to stewardship. Stewardship may initially mean putting a flower in a vase to decorate our table. But stewardship will take us beyond that to *restoration*. We now work for the restoration of what has been abused in the past.

Beyond restoration, stewardship means *serving*. As we understand that God through creation is in so many ways serving us, we will return this service with our own lives. This service will include *keeping* creation by loving and caring for what God has given us to hold in trust. And, as the generations pass, our service to creation will ultimately involve our *entrusting* others with what we have served, kept, and restored.

Christian environmental stewardship, our loving care and keeping of creation, is a central, joyful, part of the human task. As communities of God's stewards; as the Body of the One who made, sustains, and reconciles the world; our churches and our lives can be, and must be, vibrant testimonies to our Redeemer and Creator.

Thou art worthy, O Lord, to receive glory and honour, and power: for thou hast created all things, and for thy will's sake they are, and have been created.

—Revelation 4:11 GB

Postscript

Dear Reader,

I hope this book has inspired and uplifted you. I hope it has helped empower you and your friends to address the world and its environmental concerns in a healthy, wholesome way in your church, home, work, and society. I also hope you have renewed with me your awe and wonder in our Lord's creation.

No doubt, early in this book you also experienced the stress that I have felt when faced with our human abuse of creation. But we have now passed through that valley and have come to the highland of participation in the joy and delight of responding in love and gratitude to the Creator of heaven and earth. We have entered into the light of imaging God's care for creation. We are affirmed now in our joyful singing of the doxology. We are affirmed in our deep-seated hope that God's creatures of whom we sing will continue their successive generations of praise to the Creator God.

Today, I sit again at the edge of the great marsh, the magnificent masterpiece of which I am steward. And today, as they have been doing here every year for thousands of years before me, the returning cranes are again clangoring in wild song! Praise God, all creatures here below! May they continue to praise God through the coming generations. And may the Lord bless and keep you, as together we continue to keep our Lord's earth!

Suggestions for Group Session

Getting Started

Through this book we have discovered what we can do to care for God's creation. But now we have to face up to a very real problem: putting what we know into practice. This chapter explores why we might be discouraged from doing so. It identifies various stumbling blocks and one pitfall that can get in the way of our actions. It also gives us the opportunity to explore our own reasons for not acting. By so doing, this chapter allows us to clear the way to act on our beliefs as stewards of our Lord's creation, to the praise of our great Creator.

Begin this last session by joining hands and singing the doxology, "Praise God from Whom All Blessings Flow." Discuss how this doxology has taken on new meaning as you have spent these sessions looking at God's creation and creatures.

While still holding hands, pray that we will all be inspired to be faithful stewards of God's creation without being sidetracked or tripped up by distractions that steer us away from exercising what we believe. Pray for the ability to discern what is right. Pray for others too, that they might not be misled but rather guided to acknowledge and respect their Creator in thought and word and in concrete, meaningful actions.

Group Discussion and Activity

Following are many suggestions for activities that you can do in your group today. It's likely that you won't have time to do them all, so please choose those that you think are most appropriate.

From Chapter Six

1. What one stumbling block impressed you the most? How prevalent do you feel this stumbling block is in your circle of church friends?

2. What other stumbling blocks might there be to putting our creation concerns into practice?

3. Why do some people blame Christians for the environmental "mess" we are in? What does the idea of "dominion" have to do with it?

4. In the shift from awareness to appreciation to stewardship, where do you find yourself?

From Your Experience

1. "New Agers," pantheists, those who are politically correct, worldly environmentalists. . . . Given the true teachings of the Bible, how are we expected to relate to these people? Do we have any responsibility toward them?

2. To what extent should we or can we cooperate with non-Christians in creation keeping?

3. May humans pursue God's blessing of fruitfulness to them (Gen. 1:28) at the expense of God's fruitfulness to other creatures (Gen. 1:22)?

4. Do you know of any earth-spirituality people? How much contact would you want to have with such people?

From the Bible

1. Read James 1:22-25. How can this passage be applied to environmental issues?

2. Why would earth spiritualists be offended by Nehemiah 9:1-6?

3. What image of Christ do we get from reading Revelation 4:11—a living, vibrant, active Christ, or the "Christ Spirit" of the earth spiritualists?

Summary
　　Each member of the group should share one insight or impression that has made an impact on him or her throughout this study. Group members may also share one thing they hope to do as environmental stewards.

Closing Prayer
　　Pray to be disciples of the One through whom the world was made, is held together, and is reconciled. Give thanks to God for creation. Pray that the Holy Spirit will lead group members to action. And give thanks for the church of Jesus Christ, praying that its members, together with your congregation, will be the children of God for whom the whole creation awaits with eager expectation.

RESOURCES

Berry, Wendell. *The Unsettling of America: Culture and Agriculture.* New York: Avon, 1977.

Bratton, Susan P. *Six Billion and More: Human Population Regulation and Christian Ethics.* Louisville, Kentucky: John Knox/Westminster Press.

Brown, Lester, et al. *State of the World: A Worldwatch Institute Report on Progress Toward a Sustainable Society.* New York: W. W. Norton; annual publication.

Brueggemann, Walter. *The Land: Place as Gift, Promise, and Challenge in Biblical Faith.* Philadelphia: Fortress, 1977.

Daly, Herman E. and Kenneth N. Townsend, eds. *Valuing the Earth: Economics, Ecology, Ethics.* Cambridge, MA: MIT Press, 1993.

DeVos, Peter A., Calvin B. DeWitt, Vernon Ehlers, Eugene Dykema, and Loren Wilkinson. *Earthkeeping in the Nineties: Stewardship of Creation.* Grand Rapids, MI: Eerdmans, 1991.

DeWitt, Calvin B., ed. *The Environment and the Christian: What Can We Learn from the New Testament?* Grand Rapids, MI: Baker, 1991.

DeWitt, Calvin B. and Ghillean T. Prance, eds. *Missionary Earthkeeping.* Macon, GA: Mercer University Press, 1992.

During, Alan. *How Much Is Enough? The Consumer Society and the Future of the Earth.* New York: W. W. Norton, 1992.

Freudenberger, C. Dean. *Global Dust Bowl: Can We Stop the Destruction of the Land Before It's Too Late?* Minneapolis: Augsburg Fortress, 1988.

Gelderloos, Orin. *Eco-Theology: The Judeo-Christian Tradition and the Politics of Ecological Decision Making.* Glasgow, Scotland: Wild Goose Publications.

Gore, Al. *Earth in the Balance: Ecology and the Human Spirit.* Boston: Houghton Mifflin, 1992.

Granberg-Michaelson, Wesley, ed. *Tending the Garden: Essays on the Gospel and the Earth.* Grand Rapids, MI: Eerdmans, 1987.

Meyer, Art and Jocele Meyer. *Earthkeepers: Environmental Perspectives on Hunger, Poverty, and Injustice.* Scottdale, PA and Waterloo, ON: Herald Press.

Nebel, Bernard J. and Richard T. Wright. *Environmental Science: The Way the World Works,* 4th ed. Englewood Cliffs, NJ: Prentice Hall, 1993.

Thomas, W. Mark, ed. *Evangelicals and the Environment: Theological Foundations for Christian Environmental Stewardship. Evangelical Review of Theology,* [Special Issue] vol. 17(2) April, 1993. (Available from Au Sable Institute, Mancelona, MI 49659.)

Wright, Christopher J. H. *An Eye for an Eye: The Place of Old Testament Ethics Today.* Downers Grove, IL: InterVarsity Press, 1983.

Newspaper and Journal Suggestions
Christian Science Monitor
Science
Bioscience

CREDITS

Chapter One

Based upon

DeWitt, Calvin B. "God's Love for the World and Creation's Environmental Challenge to Evangelical Christianity." In *Evangelical Review of Theology,* W. Mark Thomas, guest editor. Vol. 17 (2) [special issue] April, 1993.

Chapter Two

Based upon

DeWitt, Calvin B. "Seven Degradations of Creation." *Perspectives,* February, 1989.

Chapter Three

Based upon

DeWitt, Calvin B. "Can We Help Save God's Earth?" *ESA Advocate,* April, 1990.

DeWitt, Calvin B. "Respecting Creation's Integrity: Biblical Principals for Environmental Responsibility." *Firmament* 3 (3), 1992.

Chapter Four

Based upon

DeWitt, Calvin B. "Creation's Care and Keeping: A Reformed Perspective." *Theological Forum* (Reformed Ecumenical Council) 19 (4).

Chapter Five

Based upon

DeWitt, Calvin B. "Making Your Church a Creation Awareness Center" in *What On Earth Can You Do? Making Your Church a Creation Awareness Center* by Donna Lehman. Scottdale, PA: Herald Press.

Chapter Six

Based upon

DeWitt, Calvin B. "God's Love for the World and Creation's Environmental Challenge to Evangelical Christianity." In *Evangelical Review of Theology,* W. Mark Thomas, guest editor. Vol. 17 (2) [special issue] April, 1993.